12 FREE Gifts Inside Just For You

1. From Chains to Change Success Kit (Action Assignments) from Profit Attraction Coach, Ari Squires: Page 8
2. Forgive Yourself After Heartbreak (Video Course) from America's Forgiveness Coach, Stephanie McNeal-Brown: Page 21
3. Check Your Shame Meter (Assessment) from International Speaker, Lorna Blake: Page 32
4. Change Journey Travel Log (Online Workbook) from Life Coach, Edward E. Mosley Jr.: Page 41
5. Self-Mastery Workbook (Workbook) from Coach to High Achieving Women, Nicole S. Mason: Page 52
6. Five Minute Face Course (Video Training) from Beauty Educator, Shavon Dotson: Page 64
7. 4 Step Guide to Shampoo and Prep Natural Hair (Audio Course) from Natural Hair Educator, Alisha Davis: Page 74
8. Maximizing Independence for Quality of Life (Resource Guide) from Healthcare Professional, Ronita Boullt: Page 84
9. Daddy-Daughter Forgiveness (Audio Course) from Marriage Planner, Tameishia Pigford: Page 96
10. 7 Major Pursuit of Talent Pitfalls to Avoid (Resource Guide) from Talent Manager, Rondale Alexander: Page 106
11. Rewrite Your Story (Action Guide) from Self-Love Coach, Cathy Staton: Page 118
12. 11 Ways Youth Can Become Agents of Change (Resource Guide) from Police Officer, Sherrie Johnson: Page 126

Empowered by Ari Squires

NO MORE CHAINS – IT'S TIME FOR CHANGE

Copyright © 2018 by Ari Squires
All Rights Reserved.
Scripture quotations marked (NIV) are taken from the Holy Bible, New International Version®, NIV®. Copyright © 1973, 1978, 1984 by Biblica, Inc.™Used by permission of Zondervan. All rights reserved worldwide.
No part of this book may be reproduced or transmitted in any form or by any means, electronic or mechanical including photography, recording or any information storage and retrieval system without written permission from the author or publisher.

DISCLAIMER: The purpose of this book is to educate and entertain. The author and publisher shall have neither liability nor responsibility for anyone with respect to any loss or damage caused, directly or indirectly, by the information contained in this book.
We cannot and do not make results guarantees or give legal advice.
Cover Design: Visual Conceptionz Interior Design: SheEO Publishing
ISBN-13: 978-1732570726
ISBN-10: 1732570728

For general information or other products and services, contact Ari Squires at www.AriSquires.com, info@arisquires.com

Published in the United States by
SheEO Publishing Company
526 Wolfe Street
Suite 1
Fredericksburg, VA 22401
www.SheEOPublishing.com

Printed in the United States of America

Visit www.NoMoreChainsFilm.com
to watch these transformative stories come to life.
No More Chains: Succeeding Against the Odds – Available Now
No More Chains 2: It's Time for Change – January 1, 2019 Release
Contact Orders@SheEOPublishing.com to book a screening

Dedication

In memory of my mother and father, and to those very special people who are helping me empower minds and change lives.

Table of Contents

Acknowledgements	1
About the Visionary	3
Introduction - *Ari Squires*	5

Emotional Chains

Fifty Percent of the Problem - *Stephanie McNeal-Brown*	11
Fatherless Daughter Breaks Chain of Shame - *Lorna Blake*	23
A Broken Man - *Edward E. Mosley Jr.*	33
You Were Born to Be Great - *Nicole S. Mason*	43

Mental Chains

Mindset Over Matter - *Shavon Dotson*	55
A New Love Story - *Alisha Davis*	65
Environmental Change Leads to Mindshift Changes - *Ronita Boullt*	75

Generational Chains

Daddy – Daughter Issues - *Tameishia Pigford*	87
Chasing a Ghost - *Rondale Alexander*	97
When Love Hurts - *Cathy Staton*	107
A Product of the Projects - *Sherrie Johnson*	119

Conclusion

Action Step 1	127
Action Step 2	129
Action Step 3	130
Action Step 4	131
Action Step 5	132
It's Time for Change	134

Acknowledgments

I am deeply indebted to those individuals who over the centuries stood up for change. I am also indebted to black writers and film producers and directors who courageously share our stories to bring awareness to our history and reawaken the souls of black and brown people.

Director John Singleton encouraged me not to create with the hope that people will like it. Instead he taught me to create from the depths of my soul because that is where true art lives. His words brought new life to my creative process and have freed me from doubt, fear, and rejection.

I am a product of the great Harriet Tubman who reportedly said, "But I could have saved thousands if they knew they were slaves." These two champions have inspired me deeply.

I also want to thank and acknowledge several other people in my life who worked directly with me to make this book possible. First, this book could not have been completed without the loving support of my husband, Darryl Squires. I thank him for his support in many ways. He made this book possible by keeping my life calm, peaceful, and happy.

I thank each contributor for openly sharing their stories in humility. Without your willingness to release your own chains by sharing your past and present pains, we could not assist in freeing others from theirs.

I thank Cynthia Dixon for going above and beyond the call of duty as project manager for this book series. You were part of the first *No More Chains* book anthology, and you left a powerful impression. You will always be a part of this family. Your grace, faithfulness to me and the authors, and patience are worth more than gold. Your support was needed and greatly appreciated.

K.A. Tracy for your forgiveness and coming onboard to help me see this project through from beginning to the end with editing and professional guidance and support.

I want to thank my brother Darrin Dewitt Henson for his genuine love for me and support for this movement. Your words encourage me, and your passion for seeing growth in others propels me to keep on keeping on.

I want to acknowledge Louis Penn for the book covers and Sachi for the design. Your creativity was like magic to bring the vision to life.

A special thank you to my son, Amare Squires. You inspire me just by your presence alone in this process. You always pushed me when I didn't feel like being pushed.

A huge acknowledgment to my daughter, Avanti Squires, whose soul and spirit speaks peace. You are and will always be my breath of fresh air.

About the Visionary

Ari Squires is the founder of SheEO Publishing Company, an innovative and forward thinking publishing, design, and ghostwriting company committed to creating polished and rich content books, planners, and journals by dedicated editorial and creative design teams that bring great ideas and stories to life. SheEO Publishing Company teaches authors how to market and leverage their stories and expertise for life-long profits, media exposure, and success across all genres including educational, reference, fiction, devotionals, self-help, memoirs, and autobiographies. SheEO Publishing Company also offers its signature business PUSH Planner.

Ari coaches her clients to have their work seen well beyond their local reach into media outlets. Her premier clients have been booked for local and international television appearances on Trinity Broadcast Network, FOX News Channel, the Food Network, and other broadcast outlets as well as national publications reaching millions to promote their expertise and launch their businesses. Ari's clients have reached #1 bookselling success on Amazon, and their books are available in local bookstores throughout the country.

As an accomplished business mogul, author, speaker, film, and event producer, Ari found her literary voice by writing and speaking about her personal story and how ultimate success is simply a matter of releasing one's chains to see all the possibilities. Ari's audience and readers gain valuable insight on how to create winning habits while acquiring the tools needed to stand out. Celebrated as a change agent and master motivator with an awe-inspiring voice, Ari turned her mess into the No More Chains movement through her book N*o More Chains: A Woman's Roadmap to Finding the Strength to Reclaim Her Destiny. She also produced an inspirational documentary series, No More Chains. She has been featured on the MadameNoire webzine, the Black Business Journal, Huffington Post,* Radio One and more, to showcase her passion for and expertise in business strategy, live event success, book leverage, and marketing.

Ari challenges aspiring and new authors to live their lives with purpose, bold action, and courage. She focuses on areas of personal development, mindset mastery, business coaching, heart-driven living, and success strategies and training. Ari's literary work gives her audiences with a sense of empowerment and leaves a call to action that encourages them to reach their full potential. She believes that everyone is equipped; people can do and become anything that they put their minds to. Success and money come with discipline and one decision: to live life on your own terms.

Ari is also the author of *All I See Is Possibility: Wisdom and Inspiration on Getting What YOU Want, The Mindset of a SheEO: Seven Core Principles of Creating and Sustaining Profitable Success as a Woman in Business,* and *The PUSH Planner: The Daily Strategic Business Planner Pushing Your Toward Success.*

Introduction

When I think about No More Chains and what this movement means to me, I think about when I was a slave to my chains, holding myself back from giving all I had to offer to this world because I did not believe in myself. When you are mentally stuck, lacking action when action is necessary, it manifests in becoming physically stuck. When I was mentally enslaved, naturally this "stuck-ness" created financial chains that stunted my growth and caused me to do things I had no business doing. As I vibrated at such low frequencies, my chains grew into emotional pain, and I found myself doing damage to myself and others. It took reading and educating myself—exactly what you're doing now—for the chains to fall off.

I learned that the effects of being mentally, physically, financially, and emotionally free would allow me to live the life of my dreams. I started to change the way I thought about myself and began to believe in my inner powers to take control of my life, take matters into my own hands, and realize that I was the one responsible for overcoming anything in my life. I realized the possibilities of me making a huge difference in my life and in the lives of other people. Releasing those chains and letting those strongholds go has led me to where I am now, which is mentally strong. There's nothing that I can't do! I am physically strong because I now take actions on every single thing that I know is going to make a difference in my life and others. I am financially stable, debt-free, and money just comes to me. I attract it.

I'm also emotionally stable now. I have emotional intelligence. I know when—and when not to—shut off my emotions. Being a witness to the effects of change is something that I want for everybody. It's my life's purpose. I believe it is possible for all of us to live a life with no chains, barriers, or limitations, and if we do have them, and they do come our way, it's important that we know how to overcome them and push through them. No matter what.

What I've discovered by working with people, by helping them develop and build businesses and write books and share their stories, I realize what holds us back. My friends, we are in our own way because we are stuck in our own stories. We are stuck in our fears or those childhood experiences that scared us. Or stuck in not having the right information.

I was raised by a Baptist mother who was raised by Baptist father who was raised by Baptist mother and father. For me I know their way of thinking was different from the way I saw the world as a child. I had to unlearn some things, so I could relearn what was right for me and felt good to me. In releasing my chains and stepping into my own power, I had to be okay with not being accepted by my peers—and possibly being ridiculed because of my differences—because I didn't follow the norm.

Even when it comes to my marriage, it is not typical. I don't have a marriage that most would subscribe to. Some people say that in order for a marriage to work it has to be a certain way, and that's not true. I feel like my marriage is the opposite of what they say a marriage is supposed to be, yet ours works for us.

Just because we're taught something as a child or we've been brought up to believe something, those handed-down beliefs do not necessarily have to be the same ones we carry in our personal journey. Those too are chains that we don't realize or want to believe or accept because we've been so programmed by society, the media, family, our upbringing, or in school that we forget we can question something if it doesn't feel right to our soul.

Generally, we are hesitant to do something different and don't appreciate the concept that we are the co-creators of our own lives. That doesn't take anything away from one's Creator; it just adds more substance to the decisions we make that help us better understand our power within, that help us break free from our self-prescribed chains, that help us change our lives.

Personally, I didn't get fully free until I released those chains of wanting to be accepted, following what society says is the norm. Because of that I no longer participate in holidays or celebrations that have historical socioeconomic and racial trauma to humans that I'm not comfortable with. I have vowed to dig deeper than the surface and get down to the *why?* My curiosity has caused me to do a lot of research to find out what was hidden from history textbooks. I notice that we as individuals are not questioning what's happening and why we make certain mistakes and decisions, and why we get in our own way. No, not anymore. It's time for change!

With the No More Chains movement, it is my hope that you see yourself in each of these individuals. Their stories are not going to be your stories, but they are definitely going to be similarities. In those similarities I want you to ask yourself: *How can I change too?*

I decided to do this series again because I felt that while the first series was phenomenal—we shared stories and people were inspired—we just scratched the surface of what we need to heal, collectively. So with this series we're digging deeper. We're giving you action steps on how to attract abundance to you, how to heal from your mental, emotional, and generational wounds so that whatever it looks like for you, you can release your chains.

Enjoy the stories, but please don't forget to take the steps. There's a huge difference between inspiration and aspiration. Inspiration is a feeling but doesn't do much. But aspiration can move mountains because when we aspire to do something, we make plans, set goals, and move! In order for you to change, you have to change. If you want to see change, you have to change. In order to see different results, you have to do things differently. That's what this movement is about.

Get ready to smile, laugh, cry, go down memory lane, and get angry because that's what it takes to get out of our own way, heal, and release the chains.

Ari Squires

**Please visit www.nomorechainssuccesskit.com
to receive your free No More Chains Success Kit**

To grow we must recognize the many faces of emotional chains and how they hold us back. The lethal misconception that something is wrong with us keeps us roaming in a trance of unworthiness, which saps joy, self-love and freedom right from under us.

~Ari Squires

Fifty Percent of the Problem

We were the picture-perfect family: Tall, dark, and handsome husband. Educated, powerful, petite wife. Four beautiful children—two boys, two girls—and a Chocolate Labrador retriever to boot.

Picture perfect: lacking in defects or flaws; ideal.

However, inside the home behind closed doors, it was another story. In some ways and on some days, life was good; things were perfect. But in other ways and on other days, it was a real-life horror show.

Five days a week things ran pretty smoothly, but, oh, the weekends. Most people live for the weekend. But for us, the atmosphere between my husband and me on weekends resembled a battleground in Afghanistan. Sadly, the children were the collateral damage.

It wasn't as if we were putting on a mask or being fake; we were doing what people do when there's no intervention: making due with the broken pieces. We were just surviving and doing the best we could in spite of the constant battlefield atmosphere. It seemed like we were in recovery five days a week and for two days a week, everything blew up.

I remember it just like it was yesterday. It was very early in our marriage, and we were in an argument regarding his beeper and suspicious numbers. It was very heated because this was not the first time I suspected improprieties. I was so angry that I grabbed his beeper and threw it across the neighbor's lawn.

He was so furious that he started grabbing the crystal, taking it outside, and dropping it on the sidewalk. All of my beautiful crystal was being destroyed, and he wouldn't stop. Out of desperation I called the cops. Still enraged, I picked up our biggest knife, held it in my hand, and demanded he tell me the truth.

After the cops came I told them exactly what had happened. He told his side. The cops approached me and to my surprise told me that since I was the aggressor, they had to take me in. There I was—my entrepreneur, beautiful, college-educated self from a good family—handcuffed in the backseat of a police car headed to jail!

It was surreal; I could not believe it.

After I was fingerprinted and booked, I was put in a holding cell and held overnight. Thankfully, my husband showed up the next morning, and I was released on my own recognizance. I was ordered to check in once a week. This went on for months then suddenly the charges were dropped, and I was free. But I was arrested two more times before I decided to do something about my rage. I finally submitted to God and got therapy.

My therapist was able to downgrade me from rage to anger because we change little by little. I stayed in the marriage despite the heartbreaking constant weekly dance of suspected infidelity, his denials, and me swallowing the lies.

And poof, twenty years had passed!

There was a husband trapped in a web of infidelity and a wife trapped in rage, strife, and discord. A husband who'd been beaten down and a wife who'd become bitter behind the destruction. Surprisingly, despite this crazy-making cycle, we both wanted the same thing, but we had no idea of how to achieve it. A happy, healthy, thriving marriage and family seemed impossible.

This story, however, is not about him. It is so tempting to make this issue all about him because that is what is expected in a cheating husband situation. No, I want to talk about something that is rarely talked about. Because in society, the cheated-on wife—the victim—is heralded and celebrated for her right to be angry. She is held in the highest regard for her bitterness because she is entitled to be that way. I was held in the utmost respect in my community because few knew of my secret rage and arrest record.

Even the Bible says in Proverbs 18:17 that the one who states his case first seems right until the other comes and examines him. I was continually stating my case to my friends and anyone else who would listen, and I would justify my actions with my anger, but no one was cross-examining me.

For those reasons I want to talk about the part that women play in the breakdown of their marriage. The 50 percent that no one talks about. And if you are a woman caught in the crossfire of infidelity, I want to tear down the victim in your story, so you can be victorious in your life. I want to shine the light of truth, so you can be healed.

I believe it is high time that you stop giving away your power to your husband and the people who have hurt you in your past. It's time for you to take responsibility for your part in the breakdown of your marriage because it takes two people to ruin a marriage.

You, my dear, may be 50 percent of the problem.

Take a moment and sit in that. Consider that you may have some responsibility in your relationship problems. You may not be so angry to go to jail; however, if you want to move forward with your life, if you want to be free, it is time for you to release the chains of anger, bitterness, and unforgiveness. And trust me; if I can do it, anyone can.

If I can break the chains of three generations of bitterness, you can too. When I made the decision to change my life, I became aware of things about my heritage that I had not noticed before. I took inventory of the relationship influences in my life. Did you know you can inherit more than money and possessions from your ancestors?

One of the first and primary influences in a girl's life is her mother. I evaluated my mother's life and relationship with my father. I surmised that although they loved each other and stayed married for forty-eight years until my father's death, my mother was bitter behind years of his infidelity.

Next I examined my grandmother's life. Same conclusion. She lived a life of bitterness and never recovered. I did not want my children to inherit bitterness, so I made a decision to do differently. I made a conscious choice to change my life and deal with my 50 percent.

As Dr. Phil says, I experienced *a changing day in my life* after attending the funeral of my college sweetheart. Afterward I had a conversation with my high school sweetheart. Those two occurrences were pivotal in my life and reminded me of who I am. It was a wake-up call from my former self to remember I am worthy of love. I realized how far I had fallen and allowed infidelity to change me.

I had gone from a confident, self-assured woman full of love, life, and light—I was voted most likely to succeed by my high school peers—to a shrunken, unsure, negative, complaining, town crier. Instead of taking responsibility for myself and my actions and setting boundaries, I was playing the victim in a major, debilitating way.

In the aftermath of infidelity, I'd strayed away from my sense of self. I realized that my life was not where I wanted it to be, and I was not the person I knew was trapped deep inside. I knew there was more and different for my life.

From the time I was a little girl, I always had a sense of something extraordinary inside me. I perceived greatness and importance emanating from deep within. I did not consciously hold it back, but it faded. I had allowed the cares of life to dissipate and dim my light.

In my quest for change, I conducted a painful evaluation of my life and how far I'd depreciated myself. I realized that if I did not address my self-defeat and bitterness, I'd continue to poison everything and everyone around me.

I sought God. I cried. I prayed. I mourned. I went to therapy, conferences, workshops, and Church. I went through programs and hired coaches. I read books. I listened to YouTube and podcasts. I changed my circle. I started to walk in my purpose. I discovered that the antidote for bitterness, hurt, anger, depression, and self-pity is a simple but complex solution: forgiveness.

It was time to stop licking my wounds and drowning in my continuous pity party. It was time to put on my big girl panties and live! It was time to go from heartbreak to the abundant, prosperous, and happy life that I knew was destined for and promised by God. Once I made that decision, I was able to bit-by-bit, piece-by-piece, pull myself out of that dark place. Because we change little by little.

You can make a decision too. Begin to take notice of what was is in your hands and all the broken pieces of your life puzzle. I believe that from all those shattered pieces, God can create a beautiful mosaic. Attain the energy and motivation to seek out the picture of what He wants to create. There is more for you and your life. I know for me, at times, the only motivation and strength I had to keep moving forward was faith.

At the time I had no consciousness of what was taking place, but as I reflected back it was crystal clear to me. Three things helped me heal and can work for you: a process, accountability, and community—or simply, PAC. All the components of PAC led to my transformation. I literally went from heartbreak to happy.

Now that I've received a deeper level of healing, I help women go from heartbreak to happy with my Passport to Freedom: Forgiveness Action Plan. You don't have to merely survive and live a life of misery! I say that because healing is a process, and there are levels of healing and forgiveness. But you do have to take the first step by deciding.

Just like many others I've paid a costly tuition for the knowledge I gained in my journey. It has cost some of us our marriages, delayed by years the fulfilling of our destinies, hurt some of us dearly financially, and resulted in lost opportunities and relationships.

But don't despair because you can gain much more than you've lost. You can gain a deep, amazing, and real relationship with God. You have the opportunity for teachable moments by being transparent and humble before your children. You can learn what true friendship is. And most importantly learn to accept yourself, flaws and all. All of this is priceless, and more is priceless!

Maybe your relationship is not currently in survival mode, but you sense a downward spiral, and you want to prevent it. Maybe you are in the middle of a crisis, and you want solutions. Maybe you want to ensure that your next relationship does not end the way the last one did. Or just maybe you want to cover your 50 percent. Whatever your goals, here are seven questions to help protect you from the dark hole of bitterness.

Do you recognize who you are and who you want to be? It is so surprising how many women enter relationships without really knowing who they are. Maybe it's not so much of a surprise because there is no class in school and few people are taught this in church.

And why not because to know and be known is one of our deepest desires. The few people that really know frequently arrive there via a crisis. Think about it; if you know who you are and are firm in your knowledge, you are unstoppable.

Do you take responsibility for yourself and your actions (or non-actions) in your relationship, or do you blame others for all your challenges? Creating boundaries and realizing that you are only and solely responsible for taking your power back is how you are able to reclaim your time and regain your dignity. You have to stand firm in your decisions in order to get your strength, confidence, and self-worth back. You have to own you!

What do you want in a relationship? Many times we grow up with a fantasy of what we want and how things are supposed to be. That can be a blessing and a curse. Of course we all have a type; however, you need to be mindful of what you want. As you live, learn, and grow so will your desires and choices.

Have you identified your boundaries? A boundary is a line that marks the limits of an area; a dividing line. Do you know what your limit is and what is off limits for you? Do you know where your responsibility starts and ends in a relationship? Do you have a tendency to get out of your lane? Do you allow others to get in your lane?

These are all boundary matters. Establish yours and live like you have.

What are your non-negotiables in a relationship? Are they on-point or unrealistic? If so, have you communicated them to your significant other? One of the key differentiators is your ability (or inability) to articulate, identify, and stick to your relationship non-negotiables. What are your non-negotiables?

Since relationship skills are rarely taught, most of us determine our partners simply by attraction and/or chemistry. It is a huge mistake for that to be the sole determinant. These attractions may not all be physical but can be materialistic and idealistic as well.

Are you willing and able to make responsible, hard choices if your boundaries and non-negotiables are crossed? By establishing boundaries and non-negotiables, it makes it easier to recognize a problem. Although in order to love a person rightly, you need to keep no records of wrongs; however, crossed boundaries and non-negotiables are measuring sticks. Otherwise, there could be disorder, perpetually hurt feelings, and worse—abuse.

Know your limits. Be able to decipher your needs and wants and your mate's needs and wants. If your boundaries and non-negotiables are compromised, learn to say no when you want to say yes. Stand firm.

Have you forgiven? This is the area where there is much confusion. People don't forgive for many reasons. Some are seemingly justifiable, and you may have a right to be unforgiving. However, you are hurting yourself and the people around you by living in unforgiveness. Sometimes the effects are subtle, and sometimes everyone and everything you come in contact knows: *She's bitter!*

You may have heard the saying: *Unforgiveness is like swallowing poison and expecting the other person to die.* It's so true! Your unforgiveness is a cancer, and it rots you from the inside out. It changes everything about you. Does any of this describe you? If so, is this what you want?

Forgiveness is a choice, and then the journey begins. That's the reason I developed Passport to Freedom: Forgiveness Action Plan because heartbreak-to-happy is a destination, and sometimes you need help along the journey. It's a marathon and not a sprint.

Few women fully realize the huge impact the ability to forgive can have on your happiness. Forgiving people tend to be happier, healthier, and more empathetic. On the other hand, the inability to forgive tends to make you into a woman who can't seem to stop plotting revenge or ruminating about how you've been wronged. Unforgiving people tend to be hateful, angry, and hostile, which also makes you anxious, depressed, and neurotic.

Do you want your personal and professional aspirations to reach their ultimate potential? It requires you to forgive and release yourself from anything and everything that consistently drags you down. It's not an easy task but a crucial one.

I want that for you and every living creature on the planet. Every dream that you have, I want it to come true. Every hurt, I want it healed. I want you to do and be and have everything you are destined to. Forgiveness, I believe, is the master key to unlock freedom.

It begins with you making a choice. Are you ready? Let's go!

About the Author

When a woman's partner is unfaithful, it's not uncommon for their entire life to unravel. Stephanie McNeal-Brown's passion and pleasure is to see women bounce back from this stressful experience, forgive everyone who hurt them, and live out their God-given purpose. She helps women go from heartbreak to happy after infidelity, so they ultimately have the power to live their best life.

Through her six-year forgiveness coaching journey, Stephanie discovered that it takes three things for a woman to recover from infidelity—process, accountability, and community—and a three-cord braid is not easily broken.

Her education and training include an MBA in marketing and certification in PREP, a science-based, empirically-tested method of teaching relationship education sponsored by the National Institutes of Health. Stephanie is also a licensed facilitator of Identity and Destiny, a step-by-step guide to help you find, know, and live your God-given purpose, and is certified to teach entrepreneurship to adults and children. She had previously served as a women's ministry leader and is a member of the Alpha Kappa Alpha sorority.

The mother of four—Leah, 14; Nyah, 15; Solomon, 17; and recent college graduate Harry, 23—Stephanie loves reading, writing, learning, and the adventure of travel. She is currently separated from her husband of twenty-three years and is a full-time caregiver to her mama living with Alzheimer's.

**Please visit www.forgiveyourselfafterheartbreak.com
to receive your free Forgive Yourself after Heart Break video course**

Fatherless Daughter Breaks Chain of Shame

"Mom, it's time for you to address this. Are you gonna let him do you like that? This man needs to take responsibility for his actions no matter what age he was at the time. If you don't do it, I will because it should have been addressed already. I'm going to get in touch with him and ask: *Did you have sex with my grandmother? If you did, then you're my mom's father and my grandfather.*"

And my heart ached for my twenty-one-year-old son having to feel like he needed to step in and do something to clear the air about a situation that was more than a half-century old.

It had been coming for years. After my mom's passing in 2006, I meant to do a DNA test. I got in touch with my uncle to ask if he would help me prove the man my mother said was my father—his brother—was in fact my father. He said he would.

He called me January 1, 2016, to wish me a Happy New Year and said: "You'd better do that thing quickly because I don't know how much longer I'm going to be around."

He passed suddenly almost a year later in early December 2016. I had never gotten the DNA test done.

My father's ex-wife has been in touch over the past five years to say she has a deep knowing that I am my father's child. She encouraged me to do a DNA test to prove it.

It's Time for Change

The last straw for me is my younger son getting involved. My sons deserve to know for sure who their grandfather is. I owe it to them, to myself, to the generations before and those to come to get this handled. When I dug deep to find out what was underneath the delay, you know what I found? Shame.

One of my mom's favorite sayings was: *Shame is not a load, but it could break your neck.* She would also back it up by saying: *There are some things that it's better to take to the grave with you than to talk about.*

I have an intuition that this heavy load of shame, while it didn't break her neck literally, it seeped into her bones over time causing cancer of the bone marrow resulting in her early death at sixty years old, leaving our family completely devastated from a void that can never be filled—I'm tearing up just writing about her.

I feel moved to change things. I am breaking the chain of family secrets and lies that hide scandalous things in place never to be resolved. I'm emphatically breaking the generational curse of shame that sits in bones, organs, and body parts creating disease and cutting lives short. I am breaking the chains of embarrassment and guilt that rob us of our power as I reclaim my freedom to stand as a beacon for others who want to break free.

I'm breaking the chain of shame and embarrassment locked in place for decades surrounding my paternity as if I had done something wrong to cause this. It's time to change this long-standing dysfunction that exists within families across cultural, ethnic, and socio-economic backgrounds where some people never take responsibility for their actions. It's time to change the way many families bury their heads in the sand ignoring what happened as if doing so makes it go away. I'm stepping up and inviting people to step forward and take responsibility for their actions regardless of how many decades later an incident occurred.

It's time to stop shrinking myself to fit this situation. It's time to stop playing small about it. I love Marianne Williamson's quote that I had on my website for eons:

"Your playing small does not serve the world. There is nothing enlightened about shrinking so that other people will not feel insecure around you. We are all meant to shine, as children do. We were born to make manifest the glory of God that is within us. It is not just in some of us; it is in everyone, and as we let our own light shine, we unconsciously give others permission to do the same. As we are liberated from our own fear, our presence automatically liberates others."

An ugly rift had developed between my mom and my mom's niece. My paternal uncle had endeared himself to the maternal side of my family and was long-time friends with Mom's niece. My uncle called her and said he was convinced he was my father.

Mom had been battling cancer. After it had come back full force and she was given a few months to live, her niece chastised her for not knowing who the father of her child was and for giving me the wrong brother's name when my father was someone else. My mother and her niece had a falling out which was never resolved before Mom's death because the one thing my mom couldn't stand was being shamed. Mom was disappointed in her relative, but the person she was most angry with was my paternal uncle. How could he spread such lies? And how could her relative take sides with a stranger over her aunt? How could this be happening to her when she had acted from integrity and done the right thing?

She had told me many times ever since my childhood that after she had become pregnant, she wrote a letter to my father telling him.

He responded, "Please say it's somebody else's. Say it's one of your cousins, anybody but me. I can't be part of this."

What she did was keep the pregnancy secret.

My maternal grandmother eventually found out and helped her through the pregnancy. I was lucky to have been born into my grandma's arms, but I came through with a broken heart, a defeated spirit, and a feeling of disappointment that I was somehow not good enough for my father to want me.

I wallowed in the shame of being illegitimate from as early as I could remember. Why did I have to be a bastard child who wasn't allowed to carry the name of her father because he was too young? I remembered feeling embarrassed to say who my father was when I was asked by strangers who saw my resemblance to my paternal relatives. I wanted to disappear. I used to hang my head in shame.

Many were the times when my maternal grandmother would tell me to hold my head high as if she was echoing Helen Keller, who said: "Never bend your head. Always hold it high. Look the world straight in the eye."

My mother said that shortly after I was born, my father's older brother approached her about adopted me, saying he wanted me to know him as my father. She told my uncle that she could not and would not say he was my father to protect his brother. Plus letting him adopt me didn't feel right to her. Mom said she would allow him to be involved as the uncle he is. And so my earliest and most vivid memories of having a connection to my father's family came through this uncle who stayed present in my life throughout my growing up and through many of my life events.

Having this shameful encounter with her niece and my uncle while she was ill made Mom vulnerable. She never allowed herself to cry about anything, yet she broke down and cried about it to me. I could tell she felt robbed of her dignity and integrity. I wanted to do something to resolve it. I knew there had to be a way. My mother came from an era when people had no way to prove their story. So they would pray and ask God that one day they would be vindicated.

I believe she is cheering me on from the other side to bring a resolution to this and to clear her name.

I'd had very minimal contact with my father until I arrived in Canada when I was nineteen. I had received an invitation from friends of the family to visit Canada. I had been feeling very unsafe because of the political turmoil and ongoing gun violence in the inner-city community where I lived in Jamaica. After arriving in Canada and staying with the family friends, I felt safe and wanted to make Canada my home.

I had been in touch with an immigration lawyer who explained that Canadian immigration laws would allow it if I had a close family member who was a permanent resident or citizen. I called my paternal uncle who was living in New York to let him know what I had found out. He suggested it should be fairly easy as my father was living in Canada. He shared the phone number to reach him.

When I reached my father at his office where he worked as a manager, I asked him if he would help me stay in Canada. He was hesitant and uncomfortable with my request. He said he would think about it, explaining that it would be best for me to get in touch with him at work only. He also said he couldn't invite me home as he had a wife and kids. I explained I wasn't looking for that kind of help. I wasn't even asking for money or a place to stay. What I needed was for him to fill out forms, go to the immigration office with me, and help me apply for my permanent resident status by acknowledging that he was my father.

It took repeated phone calls, weeks of frustrating moments, and months of convincing him. But he did show up with me at the immigration office when it mattered, to swear that he was my father. I remember it very well because I felt like a fly on the wall bearing witness to this.

It was extremely awkward and uncomfortable to be in the same room with him when the immigration officials asked him several times. "Are you saying you fathered this young woman when you were fourteen years old"?

And his response each time was, "Yes."

By the end of that appointment, I received my permanent resident status in Canada as if by magic. I remember shaking inside during that immigration appointment. When we got outside, it felt weird talking to him, yet I was extremely grateful. I thanked him profusely for his help in allowing me to stay in Canada. I was planning to send him a gift to express my thanks. He gave me the work address and told me to keep contact with him at his office only. I did exactly as he asked. And over the next several years I bumped into him a few times at church events.

It came as a complete shock to me when I found out that we shared the same faith and at the time he was a church leader.

That was many years ago now, and my uncle, my father's older brother, recently passed away. It felt awkward attending his funeral with all the other relatives including my father. It had been a couple of years since we had seen each other. When we said good-bye he promised to be in touch to have a meal together. He didn't keep his word which was nothing new.

I learned from one of my aunts that she recently had a conversation with my father, telling him: "It's time for you to own up that you are Lorna's father."

According to her, he's now saying he isn't my dad because his older brother took responsibility before he died.

I've called my father several times recently asking for his participation in a paternity DNA test, and he still has not said yes.

How am I taking this? Like a champion. This is what I tell myself, and I'm sharing it with you. No matter what circumstances you may have come from; no matter the pain you may have endured; no matter the shame, embarrassment, or humiliation you may have experienced, I am here to bear witness that you are nothing short of a miracle. You are not here by chance or by accident but by Divine design. Nothing about you is by accident even if the circumstances appear suspect. That was how you've chosen and were chosen to show up on the world stage in this lifetime, and the world needs you. The world needs your gift. The world needs you exactly as you are with your challenges, the pain of your past, and all that you bring to this life.

As I take a look at my life, I am who I am and can share my unique gifts with the world because of the pain I've endured. Who would I be without my story? Where would I be without the pain of my past? What would I be without the shameful, embarrassing, humiliating circumstances I have faced and continue to face but pushing through it all? These battle scars have been gifted to me to help me serve the world with dignity, humility, and a deep sense of empathy.

I'm someone who is now living my dreams after living my nightmares. I've been helping facilitate breakthroughs, empowerment, and transformation for other people for over fifteen years. I want to help you experience healing in your own life.

I've received tremendous benefit from Louise Hay's mirror exercise and have incorporated some of my own mantras and affirmations into it.

Magical Mirror Mantras

Get in front of a mirror and repeat this first thing in the morning and the last thing at night for ninety days.

To release shame

I no longer allow my past and the shame of my past to control me. I no longer allow the opinions of others to keep me playing small. I no longer allow my limiting thoughts to keep me in a box.

To release pain surrounding your birth, your paternity

I recognize that I am not the mistakes my parents made. I may have come into this world as a result of what seems to be accidental, but I am no accident. I am miraculous and phenomenal!

To play a bigger game in life

The very thing that has been keeping me playing small has been designed to raise me up bigger and more powerfully than I could ever imagine. Everything about me including my past is perfect for the work I am here to do on the planet.

To feel more confident

This is a new season, and it's got my name written on it.

Meditation to Release Pain of the Past

This meditation can provide a sense of peace and help you let go the pain of your past without struggle.

Sit in a comfortable position with your back fully supported, and allow yourself to feel your feet flat on the floor or ground. Close your eyes and take a couple deep breaths in. Slowly release the breath out. Feel the weight of your body being completely supported by the surface you're sitting on. Know that you are supported.

As you breathe in bring in wisdom, insight, and awareness. As you breathe out let go fear, worry, self-doubt. Once again breathe in and allow yourself to receive insight, new understanding, healing. As you breathe out release all distractions, stress, tension. Be fully present to this moment.

Become aware of the place in your body where you're feeling the pain/shame of your past. Notice where exactly in your body this shows up. Thank this pain for showing up so it can be released. Bring a blue light or whatever color you choose from the heavens or infinity into your crown and then direct this laser light to the exact place of your pain/shame and see/feel/sense the light dissolving this pain completely.

Observe the place where that pain was. Give thanks for its removal. Take a couple of more deep breaths and give thanks for the powerful being that you are. When you're ready, open your eyes and come back to the space/time/room where you are.

#

As someone who has gained tremendous help from counselors, coaches, and women's circles, I believe in the power of these resources to bring tremendous value to our lives. I'd like to make myself available to help you break through.

About the Author

Lorna Blake is an international speaker, award-winning author, leadership, and prosperity mindset coach, empowering thousands globally.

Please visit https://bit.ly/2MmGoUh to receive your Check Your Shame Meter

A Broken Man

Has something ever held you hostage so strongly you knew it was bad for you, but it was the answer to all of your problems? Well, meet my friend, Mr. Alcohol. He was the chain that held me in bondage for many years.

Things were finally starting to look good for me and the family. We had just purchased our dream home, I received some awesome news of being offered a government position, I was halfway done with my coursework for my PhD, and I was so happy to be retiring from the Marine Corps after twenty-one years of honorable service. And then it all started slipping away when we received the news that my mother-in-law had been diagnosed with cancer.

For years I dealt with all of my issues by using alcohol because it allowed me to forget about everything going crazy in my life.

My mother-in-law became so ill that we eventually had to find a caregiver for her during the day while we went to work. During that same time, Raquel told me she wasn't feeling well herself and was going to go to the doctor. I asked her if she was okay and she replied yes and that she would wait to schedule her appointment until later because she wanted to make sure that her mom was okay first before dealing with anything personal.

Not long after that conversation, my mother-in-law passed on March

13, 2010. In April Raquel finally went to the doctor, and the preliminary results were not good at all. She was diagnosed with a very aggressive type of cancer. The news just tore my heart completely apart. How was I supposed to tell our kids that they were losing their mom not even thirty days after their grandmother had died?

To deal with it I started drinking my problems away because I wasn't ready to accept everything that was about to happen. What was the purpose? Why was I being used, and what message was I supposed to receive from going through these horrible things all at once? I was a walking time bomb ready to explode, a broken man experiencing things that many people will never experience in their life—sudden deaths, financial stress, losing a job, and major alcohol issues. And I kept everything on the inside.

Raquel's doctor sent the biopsy off to the University of Maryland in Baltimore for analysis. After a week went by, the results came back, and we got the call to come in and discuss the results. We arrived at the doctor's office, and when he began to explain the results, my body and mind went weak as if I was outside of myself.

What do you mean she has appendix cancer? What is that?

I couldn't even move. I felt as heavy as concrete and shook my head in disbelief. I wondered how this could be happening not even a month after my mother-in-law passed away; how had this living, breathing disease showed his head in my house again?

As the doctor started rattling off the statistics I became breathless; there was only a 32 percent survival rate.

This cannot be happening.

I'm sitting there wondering what the hell this was all about. How do I bury a mother and a daughter in less than six months? We left the appointment in disbelief and returned home in complete silence, not uttering a word to each other because neither of us had the words to speak as we were both thinking about what the hell just happened.

Raquel started becoming sicker each day, and every time we went to the doctor something else was going wrong. Her feet were swollen, breathing problems, she couldn't retain any foods, collapsed lungs, unable to urinate, etc. These issues started happening so consistently that I started missing work and couldn't leave the house because of the amount of pain she was in.

I eventually got approval from my supervisor to telework so I could take care of my wife. Raquel's health diminished rapidly, and soon she couldn't even walk up and down the stairs at home. So I carried her up and down the same stairs just as I did my mother-in-law a few months before. As things progressed with Raquel, I slowly started to disengage from friends and started drinking more to avoid the reality of what was going on around me. I began to form another persona of myself that could handle everything; he smiled, he laughed, and he never cried because he couldn't show any weakness. He was like Superman.

I remember going to work one day, and it felt like I was not really present because I had so much on my mind, without any answers. When I finally gathered my thoughts enough to try and work, I got a call from Raquel's nurse saying my wife was in tremendous pain and should go to the emergency room. Speeding down the highway, I asked the Lord to heal my wife.

When we checked into the hospital, the doctor immediately informed me that Raquel's kidneys were failing, and they needed to admit her asap. During the time she was in the hospital, I started getting up at 4:00 a.m. so I could go to the hospital and spend a couple of hours with her before going back home to get the kids ready for school then head to work. I kept this routine up for about a month because it was the only way I could take care of everything and free my mind a little during the day. But I would drink to get through the tough nights and lonely moments.

One day we got a call from a doctor at the University of Maryland in Baltimore to ask if Raquel would consider heated intraperitoneal chemoperfusion (HIPEC), a procedure used to treat advanced abdominal cancers. We decided that we would try it. My wife was getting sicker by the day, and after several visits to the ER, it was time for her scheduled surgery and away we went to Baltimore. We checked in and completed all the paperwork for the surgery and were directed to the waiting room until they were ready to prep her for surgery. We talked, we prayed, we exchanged kisses, then they took her away for a fourteen-hour procedure.

Since she would be in surgery, I left to grab something to eat, take a shower, and maybe try to get some rest. But to my surprise I got a phone call about two hours later from the hospital saying that I needed to come back as soon as possible. When I arrived at her unit, the doctor was waiting for me. He explained that he had to stop the procedure because the cancer had spread throughout her body, and the only way that he could move forward would be to remove some of her major organs. I didn't understand. I thought the HIPEC procedure was a way to burn all the cancer away, so why would it not burn the cancer off her organs? Then he hit me with the most devastating news ever.

"Mr. Mosley, the problem is that the cancer has now penetrated her organs."

I was completely speechless.

Once Raquel was released from the hospital, we again drove home in almost complete silence, both thinking about our kids. How badly would the news hurt them, or would they even understand?

In the days that followed, her pain increased, and she required more visits to the ER. Trying to remain normal, we agreed that I would go to work as if nothing had happened. But as I was attending a class on October 7, 2010, my cell phone rang; it was the nurse at home. I walked out of the classroom to listen to the message that stated: I needed to come right away because Raquel wasn't responsive.

Again my heart dropped, and I raced home. I ran upstairs and found Raquel rapidly gasping for air, unresponsive. We immediately called 911 then I made some calls to ensure the kids had somewhere to go because I knew in my spirit that Raquel was leaving us that day. And she did.

As the days and months passed after Raquel's death, I withdrew and drank even more to take my pain away. The first holidays were the hardest for me and the family; we felt like we didn't have anything to celebrate. The kids asked wasn't Thanksgiving a time to give thanks and Christmas was a time for life and happiness?

So things were not going well at all. And with the loss of my wife's income, I had to make some hard decisions. And to make things worse, I had issues at work to deal with. Less than three months after burying my wife, I was terminated seven days before I would have concluded my one-year probationary period. Our new chief of staff told me that it was based on me not completing my work assignments during the time I was out from work caring for my dying wife. He further said that some important projects that were not accomplished were my fault.

I asked myself: *How can a man go from two incomes to one income to no income after being approved in writing to telework?* To top it off I started getting letters that my house was going into foreclosure.

My life was spiraling out of control. While I was trying to deal with my other issues, I received multiple DUIs within a two years' time. So now I am dealing with the DUI charges, lawyers, court fees, state requirements, and a host of other legal issues that included losing my security clearance. I was literally tired of my life; I didn't even have the energy or the will to get out of the deepening hole that I was sinking in day by day.

I remember my oldest daughter came and thanked me for not leaving; she told me that most men would have left and not cared. Those words from my daughter touched me in such a way and was a pivotal point in my life because I had just received my second DUI. At that moment I knew I was tired of all the lying and drinking. When the police asked me that night if I had been drinking, I simply replied yes and didn't even try to get out of the charges. It was time for me to change what I was doing to my family because I was all that they had. I needed to stop being selfish and change my thought process because I was about to lose everything that I loved so dearly.

Before my court date for the second DUI, I understood all the legal issues I was facing. Because it was my second offense within five years,

I was potentially looking at three to five years in prison. I prepared my family, had a guardian in place, and appeared in court. Then something happened that I had no control over: my lawyer found an error in the first DUI proceeding that violated a Supreme Court ruling and it was thrown out. So the second DUI became a firstoffense with a much shorter jail time. At that exact moment I knew my life was about to change.

I accepted the ruling from the judge, and he allowed me to report to jail after I had gotten my kids situated. Once I was placed in my cell, I chose my rack, and before I closed my eyes I noticed a cross had been drawn on the wall directly by my head. And I immediately felt the presence of God over me. By that point my drinking over the past several years had become out of control; I was about to lose everything I had worked so hard for. My parents had taught me better than that, and I shouldn't have allowed alcohol to take over my life. But drinking was my way to cope with stress and everything that was going on in my life.

I closed my eyes and started to silently cry because I knew that I was saved, and God's grace allowed me to change my way of thinking and my way of life. I knew at that exact moment that I was ready and committed to changing my life. I finally admitted that post-traumatic stress and the feeling of loss and loneliness had brought me to this point in my life. I stopped thinking of me and started thinking of everyone I had let down and hurt and what I needed to do in order to fix my situation. That's when I changed my way of thinking, and it has drastically changed my life.

In order to fix my thinking, I sat down and wrote my daily routine for about a week because I wanted to see exactly what I did and when my alcohol triggers were the highest. Once I knew what environment would cause me to desire alcohol, I was able to adjust that pattern. For instance, I knew that I desired a drink immediately after work because it had become a daily habit, so I decided to go get a smoothie immediately after work. It took about a month to change the habit.

I want to leave you with this thought: when you change your way of thinking, you will change your life forever. Everything that I went through had a reason, and the more I shared my story with others of how I made it through, the more it helped them to heal. I was able to make it through by my faith and by using some simple approaches I developed. I sat down one day and started writing a plan of action in regard to my life and was able to identify steps that allowed me to find myself, which helped me to develop my CHANGE model.

If you are ready and want to make a CHANGE in your life, I invite you to allow my company, Limitless Bounds, to support you. Even though my story may be different from yours, I'm sure you are struggling with difficult issues. You may have tried to change a bad habit, to stop drinking or being an abuser, but nothing is working. Or you may be having issues in school, a marriage, or relationships. By using my six-step CHANGE model, you'll be able to release the chain that is holding you back in order to live a happy, healthy life.

During my darkest moments when I was broken, sad, hurting, and I had no money to pay my bills after losing my job; I knew that my children needed me. They had already lost their mom and grandmother, so I needed to be strong and take care of my family. The song "My Testimony" by Marvin Sapp speaks directly to my brokenness because I made it. I didn't give up, and through my faith *I made it!*

About the Author

Edward E. Mosley Jr. is an author, inspirational speaker, life coach, change facilitator, and a Marine veteran with twenty-one years of faithful service. Having lost his wife in October 2010 to appendix cancer, Edward has developed a special approach for connecting with men of any age trying to excel in life while dealing with difficult issues of existence. He is a youth football coach, a volunteer with the Aspire mentoring program, and a guest speaker with the nonprofit Change in Action. Edward has a BA in business, an MS in human resource management and development, an MS in entrepreneurial management, and an MBA. He currently lives in Virginia and is the founder and chief executive officer of Limitless Bounds.

Please visit http://bit.ly/LBJourneyTravelLog to receive your Change Journey Travel Log

You Were Born to Be Great

"Nicky, you're not like the people you are hanging with."

Those were words that my grandmother spoke to me repeatedly throughout the course of my life. She would tell me about any person I introduced her to in a split second. Her words were always the same: *I can read a book by its cover any day!*

My response would always be the same: *Grandma, those are my friends. Everybody is not like you say they are.*

After many years and experiences, Grandma, you were right.

It is important for me to unpack this story in a way that will provide the depth of what my grandmother was trying to convey to me. I was an only child and an only grandchild. Although my parents were divorced, I was indeed a daddy's girl. Being an only child, I naturally wanted to connect with other kids. But that didn't always work out the way that I hoped it would.

I ran into lots of problems early on in life trying to get in where I didn't fit. Being an only child gave me ample opportunity to read and study more, so books became my siblings. This studious behavior only added to my problems because I was then placed in the talented and gifted class. As much as I tried to fit in and be average, it just didn't work. It would take me to almost lose my life to realize the truth of what my grandmother had been trying to tell me all those years.

I grew up assisting my grandmother with her business and was running it by the age of ten or so—ordering supplies, waiting on customers, counting the money, etc. I was my grandmother's trusted employee. Looking back, I can see clearly now that right from the start my life was set up differently from those I grew up with.

We didn't live in the community where my grandmother's business was located. She was one of two women business owners in the community. I could speak business lingo because I was exposed to business conversations and negotiations early on in life. Those unique experiences set me up for the greatness I would later embrace in my life, but I was hell-bent on hanging with average people and being accepted by them. It is amazing to have conversations with people who you grew up with and hear their perspective of you. Most of the time people see greatness in you before you see it in yourself.

When I became a teenager, I started dating hustlers. I was so naïve because I didn't even know what a hustler was. I shake my head at myself even as I type these words. So many people have walked this same road that I have been on, and it's my hope and desire that my story will cause some young person, particularly some young girl, to take a deep inventory of herself and understand that she is great and make a conscious decision to walk away from people and a lifestyle that is worlds apart from how she is being raised by parents and people who love her and have her best interests at heart. Young people, please listen to those that are in your life because everybody's story does not have a happy ending.

I continued to date hustlers for no other reason than the fact that everybody else was doing it. I don't think this was even a conscious decision as much as it was a subconscious decision because of the company I chose to keep. My grandmother was also correct in her assessment that birds of a feather flock together. It is true that we begin to pick up the habits and behaviors of those we choose to spend time with on a regular and consistent basis.

Going down that path led to being date-raped by the first hustler I decided to go out with. The funny thing is your mind can make you believe all sorts of things if you aren't careful. That is exactly why we all need wise people in our lives to guide and direct us. The reality of the situation really didn't hit me until many years later when I was in college and listening to someone else at a forum talk about being date-raped. I knew that the guy forced himself on me, but I somehow made it less of what it really was because I had agreed to go to his house. But that was how my thirteen-year-old mind processed the violation.

Sometimes it takes more than one event for people to become aware of who they really are. That is why we can't give up on people when they make mistakes consistently during their youth while trying to figure life out in a way that makes sense to them. However, there will come a time when ignoring signs and warnings lands you in big trouble. That is exactly what happened to me on June 7, 1992.

Yet again I was entertaining a hustler, knowing and understanding that we were living in two different worlds. I had graduated from college, was on my way to law school, and prided myself on being a college girl who knew how to navigate the hood in which she grew up in. Wrong thinking, wrong perspective, just wrong!

At approximately 2:00 a.m. in the morning on June 7, 1992, I was sitting in the car when two men walked up. As they approached, I looked out the rear window to see the barrel of a gun right before they opened fire, gunshots piercing the calm of the early morning. I later found out it was a hit on the guy I was with that night. Unfortunately, I just happened to be at the wrong place at the wrong time. Things certainly could have ended very differently for me, but God had another plan for my life!

As the bullets rang out, I started screaming and hollering the name of Jesus, and it felt like some force literally picked me up and pushed me down the street. I don't remember opening my driver's side car door. It felt like an out-of-body experience. When I came to myself, I was running down the lonely, dark street. There weren't any other cars in sight. No one was out there to help me as I ran for my life, still hearing the gunshots behind me. I never looked back to see if anyone was chasing me. I just kept running for as long as I could and as far as I could. That turned out to be only two blocks away from where my car was parked. The gunshots were still going when I suddenly began to feel like I had been shot. My heart was racing at an unbelievable speed, my legs got weak, and I could barely breathe.

I was walking alongside the front porches along the street feeling faint when I looked up and saw two people on their front porch. The only words I could get out were, "They shot him. They shot him."

They didn't ask me any questions. They just told me to come inside and lie down on the floor. I didn't get their names, but I provided a description to my mom. My stepsister verified the address and the description of the people who helped me that morning.

I told them I was trying to make it back to my stepsister's house, but

I just couldn't run any longer. The man called 911 and my stepsister, and the woman kept talking to me in a calm voice, assuring me that everything was going to be alright. In a matter of minutes, my stepsister was at their front door watching me come out of the house.

I desperately wanted to go back to the scene to let the police know that it was my car my friend and I had been sitting in. When the police and paramedics arrived, they didn't find me, but they found my purse in the car, the keys in the ignition, and one shoe on the floor in front of the driver's seat.

Everyone in the neighborhood knew that was my car, and someone called my mother to tell her that they didn't know if I was dead or not, but my car was shot up, and the guy in the car was dead. My mother never fully recovered from that telephone call, but that's another story for another time. That was a day that changed the very course of my life and the lives of those who loved me the most.

For many years after this life-altering event, which took place less than a month after I had graduated, my life seemed to be one big blur. What was once normal became foreign. The people I called friends were nowhere to be found. My grandmother was correct, and my life as I knew it was totally shut down! Soon thereafter, I found myself living on the run because I wasn't sure if the people who shot my friend were going to be looking for me.

I also wasn't sure whether my friend's family members were going to come looking for me, especially since he died in the car and I did not. I was faced with rumors that I set him up and that was the reason I didn't die. Of course that was a complete lie. I wouldn't know where to begin to have someone murdered. I was a law-abiding citizen with a dream in my heart to go to law school to help people who were victims of crime. This was indeed a huge twist of events in my life that I did not count on and was not prepared to handle.

I suffered a great deal emotionally, physically, and mentally. I couldn't sleep for months. I was barely eating, so I dropped a tremendous amount of weight. I couldn't concentrate, so my four-year-old son bore the brunt of that aspect of the ordeal the most. He and I had just walked across the stage together when I graduated from Howard University. Then he encountered and experienced a despondent, depressed, and detached mom. Everyone who loved me the most suffered too. When I did finally make it back to work, I would show up with my hair in shambles, looking disheveled, and feeling lost and uncertain. Detectives were coming to my job and my home trying to speak with me. I was mentally exhausted, embarrassed, and just downright in shock. It took me years to get my life back on track.

I was a witness at the murder trial. I knew the person who was arrested for my friend's murder. We all grew up in the same neighborhood—sort of. Even though we didn't live where my grandmother's business was located, since I spent most of my time there I considered myself from that particular neighborhood. Wrong thinking, wrong perspective, just wrong!

It was apparent that I was not considered a member of the neighborhood, at least from my vantage point, since the perpetrators chose to shoot my car up. It would be one year and several months before the prosecution was ready to bring the case against the perpetrator. They only apprehended one shooter. During that time, I was the recipient of a scholarship to a paralegal program. My dreams of starting law school were shattered, so I had to do a slow climb back to the point of applying again. As I look on it now, the fact that I was rejected nine times before being admitted was God's grace, because I wasn't mentally stable enough to focus on a rigorous law school program, trying to raise my son, and trying to put the pieces of my life back together.

While attending the paralegal program, I met an attorney teaching one of the courses. I asked her if I could serve as her intern, and she said yes. We were working at the courthouse one day, and I noticed a family member of my murdered friend. I hadn't told the attorney about what was going on in my life, so I did not want the cousin embarrassing me in front of my teacher and the many people in the courthouse that day.

So as the cousin was walking towards me, I am literally spilling my guts about everything that had transpired in my life the previous year. The attorney was overwhelmed and so was I. By the time the cousin was close enough to speak to me, my teacher and I were both looking shell shocked. The cousin smiled widely and told me how glad she was that I was alive and fine and doing okay. Her words left me speechless and weak at the knees because my adrenaline was preparing for a battle. She hugged me and walked away. I had to run to the restroom because I could not stop the torrential rain of tears flowing down my face. I wept and wept in the bathroom until I felt like there wasn't any water left inside of me.

After I gathered myself my teacher and I were able to discuss the matter. I told her that I was scheduled to go before the grand jury the next day.

She immediately offered to serve as my lawyer. She represented me without a fee. I had not even thought about retaining counsel because in my twenty-three-year-old mind I wasn't guilty, and I hadn't done anything wrong.

Again, wrong thinking, wrong perspective, just wrong.

You never go to court without representation! I went through the grand jury proceeding, which was very stressful for me. The prosecution indicted the perpetrator. The day the trial was scheduled to start, he pled guilty. This meant that I would not have to offer my testimony again. The stress of the grand jury proceeding was enough for me!

As the years went by, I slowly put my life back together. I gave my heart to the Lord. I began serving in my local church. I eventually was accepted into law school on the tenth time that I applied. I passed the bar exam and became a practicing attorney. I accepted my call to preach. I started a ministry to empower and encourage women. I started a business. I have written books. I have traveled internationally to preach and conduct leadership training.

The perpetrator served his time in prison. Nineteen years later, I saw him at my youngest son's school. His sons attended the same school unbeknownst to me. When he saw me, he made a quick move toward me, and I wasn't sure what to do. I guess he could see the look on my face because before he got very close, he started apologizing to me. He said that he wanted to ask my forgiveness for what he did that fateful morning that our paths had crossed. He explained that he took advantage that I happened to be there that morning with my friend in the car, vulnerable to attack.

You see, when there is greatness in your life, God will do whatever is necessary to ensure that you accomplish what you were sent to the earth to do. A few years after that life-altering event, my mom shared with me that she went back to the house of the people who helped me that morning. She wanted to say thank you. The person who answered the door told my mom that no one by those descriptions ever lived there. Well, those people were angels assigned to my life. I am sure of it, and no one can make me doubt it.

Your greatness will cause miracles to happen in your life to get you to the place that you were destined to be from the beginning. You were born to be great; show up great!

About the Author

Nicole S. Mason is known as the leader's leader and is sought after for her wise counsel and effective leadership strategies. She serves as coach and confidante to high-achieving women in the marketplace and in ministry. Aligning her leadership acumen and her faith creates a powerful combination for those who retain Nicole to help them to make strategic decisions and power moves.

Nicole is a licensed attorney in the State of Maryland and is the founder and chief executive officer of Strategies for Success, a speaking and leadership coaching company. In this capacity she works with female leaders and executives to pull out what is already inside of them through the powerful practice of coaching and speaks professionally on the topics of confidence, how to show up great, and the power of you, to name a few.

She is also the host of her own radio program, the *Nicole Mason Show*, on the Radio One Network that can be heard around the world. The show highlights powerful women sharing their stories of trials to triumph as encouragement to other women that trouble really does not last.

Nicole has also served on nonprofit boards and has been the recipient of many awards for her ground-breaking and trailblazing work as the only female African-American leader to serve in her position in the organization where she is currently employed. She has been featured in numerous magazines and newspapers and on more than twelve media outlets. Nicole serves as an ambassador for the American Heart Association, bringing awareness to heart disease and its impact on women. She is an example to women that you can do whatever you set your mind to do. Nicole is a natural-born encourager, and if ever in her presence, you will definitely feel the impact of her encouraging spirit!

**Please visit www.selfmasterywithnicole.com
to receive your Self-Mastery Workbook**

You start living the moment you decide your life is your own with no apologies or excuses. No one to lean on, rely on, or blame. The gift is yours to make up your mind and decide that you are responsible for the quality of your life. This is when you break the chains to become free. Many of us are just one decision away from the most amazing journey of our lives.

~Ari Squires

Mindset Over Matter

At a very young age, I knew that the world was much bigger than my hometown, Milwaukee, WI. Even though I grew up in a very rough neighborhood, one where dreams often died with the dreamer on those cold, mean inner-city streets, I knew that I had to find a way out; both my dreams and my life depended on it.

Have you ever wondered *Why me?* especially when it seems like one thing after another, with no end in sight to the pain, the suffering, the depression, and the guilt? I've asked God the *why me?* question more times than I care to share, and if I'm honest, there was one point in my life where I just figured I was paying for every bad word, action, or thought that had ever entered my mind. I grew up in a household where the Holy Bible was the law, and for years my religion told me that when God was angry with me, He would take out His wrath on me, so I just chalked up my circumstances to a God who was in constant fury with me.

As a little girl, whenever I would do something bad, I would get my mind set and prepped for the bad thing that was going to inevitably happen to me as a result of my disobedience. That mindset plagued my life for years, and it wasn't until my thirties that I was able to break the chain that bound me to believe I would always be a product of my circumstance, that I did not have the power to change the path that my life was going down.

When chains are broken and mindsets are changed, you start to realize that the sky really is the limit for what you can do, the life you can live, and the impact that you can have on this world. Now that I'm able to look back over the things that bound me and almost broke me, I understand that it wasn't God taking out His wrath on me; instead, I was making deliberate choices to keep myself in the sunken place. The shift for me happened when I decided to stop living my life according to what others believed I could or should be, and I started to believe that my dreams were simply goals waiting to be accomplished.

Born and raised on the northside of Milwaukee, Wisconsin—yes, there are black people in Wisconsin—I grew up believing that gun violence, drugs, and poverty were normal since that was my reality every day. As the youngest of five children, I always felt like a unicorn in my family; I never quite felt like I fit all the way. I was the ugly duckling, the one with the smartest mouth, and the one with the biggest dreams. Growing up, I didn't quite realize that we were living in poverty because I had never met anyone who was living above and beyond how we were living. It was common to see street corner drug deals, police raids of the neighbors' homes, and RIP T-shirts adorned with the faces of the latest victims of gun violence plastered on them.

My first real understanding of death happened when I learned that my eleven-year-old next-door neighbor was gunned down by a stray bullet in a drive-by shooting. It was a shock to my system because my young mind couldn't comprehend how someone my age and so innocent could be gone so tragically.

Unfortunately, that wasn't the last time I would have to cope with a violent death. It became so common that it was numbing; it became just another T-shirt to rock—well, until it happened on my front porch. Watching my eldest brother laying on our front porch desperately and unsuccessfully trying to hold onto life was the final straw for me. I couldn't numb that pain. It wasn't fair, and I wondered what bad thing my family had done to receive such wrath from God.

That was the moment I knew God was watching, and He wasn't pleased, so I vowed to get my life together and do whatever was necessary to stay in His good graces. I turned my life around. I was going to church faithfully, praying every chance I had, and working hard to keep temptation away. And being a freshman in college, there was temptation surrounding me daily. My method worked for a while, at least until I ended up eighteen years old and pregnant six months after my brother had died.

I knew that God was punishing me for *one* reckless night I had. For a fleeting moment I thought I had made it. There I was, a black girl from the inner-city of Milwaukee, attending one of the best universities Wisconsin had to offer—for free. But it was clear to me that it wasn't in the cards for me to get away from the 'hood. I had a victimization mindset at the time, and I was blaming everything around me for the things happening to me.

I spent the remainder of that summer packing up my belongings and saying my goodbyes to the city that had given me my first dose of adulthood. During my last night on campus, I took a long walk on the silent streets of Madison. I kept trying to convince myself that leaving the university and moving back home was for the better. Although the argument was compelling in my head, my heart wasn't so convinced. I hated home and everything that it stood for. I felt like I was settling for second best when I had a chance to experience the absolute best.

Once again I figured God must have been mad at me. I knew that I would go home and work some second-rate job, go to a second-rate school, and live a second-rate life. I was better than that—at least I thought I was. I had no one to help guide me in making the best decision for my life. My family had convinced me that moving back home would allow them to support me more, and I needed all the support that I could get. So I guessed it just made logical sense. I went home and hoping to relieve some of the anxiety I was experiencing, I picked up my pen and allowed my heart to guide me.

Dear daughter,

It's going to be just you and me from here on out, and that's okay. You've made me realize that I am worth so much more than I've been settling for. Yes, I'm eighteen, a college dropout, and pregnant, but I refuse to feel ashamed anymore. I'm ready to step into my greatness because now I understand that my greatness is tied to your future.

Love always,

Mommy

Maybe it was the breakthrough I needed, and with a newfound sense of purpose, things were about to get better. I was no longer living just for me, and I knew that every decision I ever made needed to be done for the sake of my unborn child. My mother told me that my life was not my own anymore, that I needed to grow up and be the mother this little girl deserved. I internalized those words and lived by them.

I went back to Milwaukee with more than just purpose; I went back with a plan. I lived at home with my parents until my daughter was seven months old. Determined that I would not let her grow up the same way I did, we packed up the few items I owned, and I went back to college. It was hard but not impossible. I slept when I could, studied while she was in daycare, gave up everything that made college fun, and dedicated myself to finishing school within the next four years so I could make something of myself for my daughter.

I finally got it right, and in December 2007 I walked across the stage with my three-year-old by my side and received my degree. I believed the hard part was finally over, and I was ready to step into the good job I knew would finally come since I had done right by my daughter, beat the odds, and got that degree.

Three years later I was working for a little more than minimum wage, on welfare, and on the brink of eviction for the millionth time. My depression had gotten the best of me, my insomnia was at an all-time high, and I was fresh out of motivation.

After living my life the right way—being the good mother and sacrificing it all for the sake of my daughter—I was ready to give up. I was spending my nights sitting in the bathroom on the floor, crying in the dark. I couldn't let my daughter see how broken her mother was and how much of a failure I had turned out to be. I was tired of hearing what mothers are supposed to do and how much mothers are supposed to sacrifice for their kids. I was all out of energy to give; motherhood was literally sucking the life out of me.

It's Time for Change

It was the moment I found myself contemplating the value of my own existence and realized that I was over trying to fit into everyone's perfect idea of what I should be. I was fed up with believing that God was constantly punishing me for my transgressions. I was tired of finding myself broke and almost evicted month after month. I had finally gotten to the point where I said: *I quit trying to be the perfect daughter, the perfect mother, the perfect idea of success.* It wasn't working, so I was ready to try a new mindset. The moment I decided that I no longer wanted to live my life afraid of disappointing my parents, my daughter, and God, is when I finally found the freedom I had been searching for my whole life.

I was tired of being bound to the mindset telling me to give more of myself to everyone other than me. I was ready to start discovering my own truth and figure out what my purpose really was because it had to be more than just being a mother. I stepped out on faith in a major way and quit my minimum wage job, moved to one of the most expensive places in America, and prayed that interviews turned into steady employment.

I always had an affinity for makeup; it was my therapy when I was battling depression. With a $100 investment, I decided to launch my own beauty career as a freelance makeup artist. I didn't know the first thing about running a business, but it didn't matter. It was something that was in my heart ever since my first makeup job at the Chanel counter when I was in college, and I was ready to turn this hobby into a hustle.

I was finally doing the things that served me, and it scared me, but I didn't care. I was a businessowner, something that no one else in my family could say, and I was proud but not because I was the first to do it. No; I was proud because it was the first step in building a new legacy.

Determined to overcome fear and self-doubt, I took the little money I had and invested it back into my business every chance I got. I invested in business coaches, personal development mentors, makeup workshops, beauty books, classes, and webinars. In an industry full of beauty professionals, I was determined to figure out my niche—the one thing that could help me stand out—and serve the clientele I really wanted to serve.

While I loved makeup and providing beauty services to my clients, I also knew there was a higher calling to my life. I knew there was a way I could take my pain, hurt, depression, anxiety, tribulations, and triumphs to impact the masses. I began to focus on teaching my clients the importance of taking time for themselves. I knew that there were women out there who were facing some of the same struggles I had once faced: giving too much of myself to others and never taking time to maintain myself. I began sharing my mediation tips, my podcast suggestions, my book list, and my fifteen-minute beauty routine with anyone who was willing to listen.

On this journey to being my best self, I've learned that the mind is one of the most powerful tools a person can have. Your thoughts turn into actions, decisions that are responsible for growth or your demise. Everything starts with just a thought. If you think you don't have enough time, then you will never have enough time. If you believe that you have no value, then others won't believe you have value either.

I've determined that my goal in this life is to educate, empower, and inspire women, and through my business I help women heal from their past hurt and traumas by teaching them how to tap into their full feminine power and live their best life through daily self-care and self-love. It's time to stop putting everyone else first and to stop trying to fit into other people's expectations of what your life should look like. Own your power, your creativity, your uniqueness, and your dreams. Someone else's breakthrough is tied to freedom. If you're unsure of where to start, use these three tips to help start releasing your own chains that are holding you down

Protect your energy and your space. For you to really start shifting your mindset, you will need to learn how to protect your energy and the thoughts that you allow yourself to think. Start to monitor the content you are consuming because that content will influence how you think and how you feel.

This may sound simple and petty, but one of the first things I cut out of my life was anyone's social media pages that made me feel horrible about myself. That change had nothing to do with those people, but it had everything to do with where my mind went when I would run across those social media pages. I cut out the content that was leading me to compare my life with theirs. I started to only tap into social media pages that were empowering, uplifting, connecting, and encouraging. That minor change made an enormous difference in my life.

Take time for yourself every morning. I truly believe that if you look good, you will feel good and vice versa. I believe in starting every morning with a morning meditation or morning mantra while I spend fifteen minutes implementing my beauty routine. Even on days when I may not have fifteen full minutes, I spend at least five minutes affirming my beauty, my intelligence, my worth, and my goals as I take the time to practice some self-maintenance. I love to show up fully for myself every day, and that means making sure that I put my game face on every day. A little concealer and some lip gloss makes a world of difference to my confidence.

Start small and celebrate your wins. Set goals for yourself daily, and remember to celebrate the progress you've made towards those goals. If you have a goal to spend fifteen minutes on your beauty routine in the morning but could only carve out five minutes, celebrate that you took five minutes for yourself today. We get so caught up in winning the war that we forget to celebrate the little battles we overcome daily.

Start your business, write your book, take that trip, and remember to congratulate yourself every time you get one step closer to those goals. Don't focus on how long it takes you to get to the goal; be proud of yourself for being willing to work towards it.

About the Author

Shavon Dotson is a professional makeup artist and beauty educator who specializes in creating a natural beauty look by focusing on glowing skin that doesn't feel heavy or greasy. She believes in the healing power of makeup and the power of touch. She uses her talents to create a serene and calming environment for her clients that allows them to get into a positive space, so they feel like they can conquer the world. But makeup isn't all she's made of; she's always had a passion for empowering and inspiring women through her beauty education courses.

Shavon combines her love for makeup and her expertise in program development to create content with tangible outcomes customized to fit the need of the client. Through her understanding of the importance of both mindset and skill set in her business, she has been working tirelessly at creating the life of her dreams and is dedicated to educating, empowering, and inspiring other women to do the same.

Please visit http://bit.ly/fiveminutebeauty
to receive your Five Minute Face course

A New Love Story

Every adversity is a blessing in disguise, provided it teaches some lesson we would not have learned without it.
— *Napoleon Hill*

I grew up in Little Rock, Arkansas. My life started out as what some might seem a fairytale because in the black community at that time there weren't too many homes where both parents were college graduates. My parents, like those of many of my friends, were married and worked together to raise their children. I had two sisters, and we lived in a lovely home.

Then things started to unravel.

When I was an adolescent, I noticed my parents' idyllic relationship developing cracks. They started having disagreements, which advanced to arguments. Soon they were shouting at each other, and our household became full of tension. As the eldest I used to comfort my two sisters although I was just as upset as they were at the sound of our parents' raised voices.

Eventually my mom decided she couldn't take it anymore, and she left—by herself. Even nowadays it's not too often that fathers get custody of their kids, but back then it was really rare. In a reversal of the usual situation, it was my mom who paid child support to my dad and he who made all the decisions regarding our day-to-day lives: what clothes we wore, what movies we got to see, etc. Although Mama didn't live far away, we rarely got to visit her; it was as if she'd lost interest in us.

At twelve years old—my sisters were just eight and six when Mama left us—it was hard to cope with not having her around. I'll never forget the day my period started, and I had to tell my daddy. It was embarrassing for both of us. My daddy loved us in his own way, and he provided for us. But he wasn't an affectionate man and didn't give the hugs and kisses I craved.

Starved for both attention and affection, I started acting out. My grades dropped, and I got into fights at school, especially whenever I heard somebody talking about my mama having left us. At that point in my life, I just didn't care about anything. My sisters had a hard time too. Nobody likes being the odd man out, and *everybody* had a mama—everybody except us.

My uncaring attitude wasn't helped by my heavy workload. Daddy needed help keeping the house and us looking nice, and as the eldest sibling it fell on me to help with cooking, cleaning, laundry, even braiding my sisters' hair. I resented the work I had to do and sometimes lost my patience with them.

Eventually we adapted to the absence of our mother, at least on the outside. But inside all three of us were angry at her for leaving us. Maybe it wouldn't have been such a big deal if we'd been boys, but as girls we really needed her. My dad, perhaps recognizing our need for feminine influence, began seeing another woman and married her shortly after the divorce came through. My stepmother was a good woman who took over running the household and made life more pleasant for us, but having a mother figure in the house isn't necessarily a substitute for a mother's love—at least for me it wasn't.

Being younger, my sisters listened to our stepmother better than I did. I never stopped longing for my mother's attention, and I decided that when I turned eighteen, I would seek her out and try to build a relationship with her. It took me many years to forgive her for not being there emotionally through my teenage years when like most girls, I had worries and doubts about my appearance and my attractiveness to boys. Eventually I did forgive her, and I was able to get my sisters to do the same.

Once I had children of my own, I was determined to always be there for them. I understand that kids don't come with instruction manuals; parents have to use their best judgment. I always felt my mother made a serious mistake by leaving us behind, but I came to the conclusion that just because I didn't understand my parents' behavior doesn't mean I love them any less. I also felt that I would learn from their mistakes and be a better parent to my own children.

Eventually I took control of my emotions and got my life back on track and not a moment too soon because major challenges lay ahead. I went to a trade school and studied cosmetology, but during my last few months there, I began losing my hearing, a terrifying experience for a twenty-one-year-old. Then just before cosmetology graduation I learned I was pregnant.

Right before graduation my best friend and I shared an apartment in a rental property my father and stepmother owned. In a crazy coincidence she got pregnant about the same time I did. I kept my pregnancy secret as long as I could, but eventually my father found out and evicted us. My best friend moved back in with her parents, but my father wouldn't let me do that; he said I was a bad influence on my sisters. I moved in with my baby's father, but after we fell behind on the rent, we got evicted. After graduating cosmetology school, my boyfriend's hours got cut from full- to part-time, we didn't have much money. We ended up moving in with his family.

My hearing was getting worse, and after my baby was born, I became completely deaf in both ears due to otosclerosis, a condition where bone grows in the inner ear. Fortunately, Arkansas Rehabilitation paid for the surgery on one of my ears, so I only wear one hearing aid instead of two.

I once read that the ears are our intake valves. The sounds they absorb feed our minds and can be converted into creative power. We learn nothing from talking, but there is no limit to what we can learn by listening. I thank God for allowing me to go through this challenge at such an early age because it gave me the awareness to keep my mouth closed and be a better listener.

You can't respond to negativity if you can't hear it. Not being able to hear rumors and gossip freed me up to concentrate on being the best person I could be. A hearing loss, at least to me, is not as devastating as the loss of eyesight or a limb. With my hearing aid I'm able to be fully functional and don't consider myself disabled.

Losing my hearing is just another example of some things being out of my control. Those who learn to adapt to life's curveballs are the ones who will succeed. Living with hearing loss has both challenges and advantages. And that is pretty much how life is. You always want to find the advantages in any situation and focus on the positive side of the issue, and most of the time the negative will reverse itself. Don't let your disadvantages control the way you want your story to end.

Your only limitation is the one which you set up in your own mind.

— *Napoleon Hill*

Looking back on my younger adulthood, I spent a lot of time being angry, and I made some terrible decisions. In hindsight I believe there's a direct correlation between the two. I was angry about blossoming into womanhood. I was angry about my father's lack of affection and his refusal to let me come home when I was in trouble. I allowed my anger at my mother to prevent me from fully accepting the love my stepmother offered me. And I was angry about suffering hearing loss at such a young age. I believe that I made the subconscious decision to just let life happen and not do anything to steer it in a positive direction.

I married my children's father after our second child was born, knowing he was hooked on drugs and alcohol. Now I see the futility in trying to improve the life of someone who has no interest in making things better. I realize I should have put the energy I invested trying to get him clean and sober into improving life for my children and me. In the wake of my failure to stop my husband's substance abuse, I found myself getting angry then feeling nothing at all as if I was dead inside.

My internal battle was obvious to others; my family and friends would tell me I was a mean person who said hurtful things. That behavior stemmed from my feelings of hopelessness, of being stuck in a life that would never improve. One day I just broke down, asking myself what was wrong with me; there was no answer, just a raging desire to improve my life. I truly feared for my sanity, and I decided to utilize the resources at the public library to get help. That's where I discovered the book *Transform Your Thinking and Transform Your Life* by Dr. Bill Winston.

> *God wants to bring a radical transformation in your mind and heart so that you can have supernatural courage in the face of insurmountable odds.*
> — Dr. Bill Winston

I discovered that the good thing about our brain is that it willingly adopts any changes we bring about in our thought patterns. Our actions are the manifestations of our thoughts. How we think shows through in how we act. Attitudes are mirrors of the mind.

In other words, it's up to you to change the direction of your life. *You* have to stand up for your own sanity. *You* have to break free from past hurts and disappointments. *You* have to believe your life can be better then take action to *make* it better.

That knowledge has changed the way I am raising my children and how I communicate with them. I've made more time to talk with them. I often ask how they feel about current situations. I ask about what challenges them, what they're concerned about. I encourage them to share their opinions in a respectful manner. Most of all I find myself hugging them and telling them I love them nearly every day, giving them the affection missing from my own childhood. My newfound knowledge has taught me to seek happiness and contentment in the present.

> *How simple it is to see that we can only be happy now, and there will never be a time when it is not now.*
> — Gerald Jampolsky

When we are under pressure, we find out how strong our resolve is, how much we can withstand. We learn what we can push through and what empowers us. My life-changing experience has empowered me to push through any challenge and to work toward my goals, knowing it is possible to attain them.

My professional goal is to empower black women through teaching them techniques to make their natural, textured hair more manageable, to give them knowledge about the needs of their hair. Many women aren't aware of how to get their hair healthy again and keep it that way. As a salon owner and hairstylist with seventeen years' experience, I help women get control of their hair, learn to love its kinky texture, and to nurture it. My love of hair gift has empowered me to help women discover ways to enjoy a new, natural lifestyle, so they don't have to panic if it suddenly begins to rain. My transformational hair programs will release old behaviors and beliefs black women have held for years pertaining to themselves and their hair. Once this happens they will find a new love and create a new hair story.

Start creating *your* new love story.

> *To activate others, you must activate yourself; to be enthusiastic, you must first be enthusiastic yourself.*
> *— David J. Schwartz, Ph.D.*

Self-Empowerment Tools

    Try my hair-love affirmations:
    I love my hair.
    I love the texture of my hair.

I love the behavior of my hair.
I love the color of my hair.
I love the style of my hair.
I love myself.
I am beautiful…………………………

Quotations that help me release my emotional chains

Don't wish it was easier, wish you were better. Don't wish for less problems, wish for more skills. Don't wish for less challenges, wish for more wisdom.
— *Jim Rohn*

Principle: Knock a challenge down with positive wishes.

What daily discipline can keep you strong?

We are not going to succeed in everything we attempt in life. That's a guarantee. In fact, the more we do in life, the more chance there is not to succeed in some things. But what a rich life we are having! Win or lose, we just keep winning.
— *Susan Jeffers*

Principle: Practice asking and listening.
What motivates you? How can you be a better listener?
Principle: The magic of thinking big.
What is your biggest magical desire?
Principle: Stretch your vision.
How can you add value to your life?
Principle: Don't let old traditions paralyze your mind.
What new ideas can you create for self-improvement?

The above tools can be used to think creatively and improve the quality of your goals. These tools will recondition your thinking and prepare you for success. I hope that sharing my story will free someone from being paralyzed, chained to unwanted circumstances. Fall in love with yourself again; make a habit of turning every defeat into a victory, learning from your mistakes, and moving on. It is possible to salvage something from every setback. Change your story to create a new love story!

About the Author

Owner of Real Natural Salon, Alisha Davis has been dubbed the Naturalogist due to her passion to teach women and children easy solutions to achieving and maintaining natural, healthy hair. She discovered her vocation as a child braiding her little sisters' hair and helping them feel confident about their natural tresses.

Her innate talent soon grew into a fifteen-year cosmetology career and natural hair care line, Real Natural Solutions, which has propelled Alisha to the top of her field with clients, bloggers, and media outlets alike clamoring for her expertise on how to maintain her natural hair techniques in between salon visits.

Alisha's simple yet modern approach has made her a key stylist and trainer in the natural hair industry. Her ability to create moisturized, shiny hair and beautiful, soft waves empower women to love their hair and keep her training classes filled and in demand.

And the mindset she shares helps clients not only love their hair but have the confidence to love who they are from the inside out, the first step toward personal and professional success. Alisha resides in Little Rock,

Arkansas, when she is not traveling the country doing salon makeovers, natural hair technique classes, and one-on-one hair assessments.

Please visit www.freegiftfromalisha.com to receive your 4 Step Guide to Shampoo and Prep Natural Hair

Environmental Change Leads to Mindshift Changes

When I was fifteen, my parents moved us from the projects of the inner city to the suburbs. For the first time I would attend public school. In our old neighborhood my brother and I were the only ones who went to Catholic school. My classmates there had broader experiences and easier access to engage in typical teenager activities because they had transportation. My classmates also got to do things like go on vacation to visit relatives in other states during the summer. My brother and I were limited to where we could go because my parents didn't have a car. My dad was legally blind, and my mother didn't learn to drive until later in life. So we got around on public transportation or depended on family and friends who had transportation.

I did have friends at school, and they liked hanging out with me in my neighborhood just sitting out on the porch or in the courtyard engaging in people-watching and sharing idle neighborhood gossip. It was exciting for my friends who were not used to living in a busy urban area where something was going on at all hours of the day and night such as spontaneous block parties, random fighting, and occasional gunshots.

On the other hand I preferred going to my friends' neighborhoods because it was much quieter. Plus their parents had cars and took us all over the city to shopping centers and movie theaters. For them these were short drives, but for me to get there, I'd have to take two buses and plan on more than an hour's travel time each way. Those same transportation issues prevented me from participating in after-school activities, and I felt a little jealous of my friends in the projects who lived much closer to the public high school and were able to join athletic teams and clubs.

I'd been born with a port wine birthmark that covered one side of my face that I'd been relentlessly teased about as a child, which left me almost painfully shy. When my parents told my brother and me that we'd be moving and going to a new public school, we were both crushed; we'd dreamed of going to the local high school with our friends from the neighborhood, me in particular because I already knew the kids, and they knew me (and my birthmark). We received a happy surprise when the kids at our new high school considered us hip because we were from the city. I was so busy socializing with my new friends, trying to keep in contact with my old ones from the projects, and finally getting to attend school functions that I had little time for studying.

By my junior year I had cut down on all that socializing and hung mostly with three new friends: a girl I had several classes with, her sister who was one year behind us, and her sister's friend, also a year younger. The four of us ate lunch together every day. All three of them were honor students, and as I hung out with them, my mindset began to change. I started paying more attention in my classes, turning in higher quality homework assignments, and my grades started to improve. My initial motivation was not wanting my new friends to think I was stupid, but their excitement about the new things they learned became as infectious as the flu.

Before I knew it I also became eager to do well in school and for the first time found myself thinking about my life after graduation. My friends all planned to attend college and pursue good-paying careers. I began to see possibilities I had never thought of or discussed with friends from my old neighborhood. Their only interests seemed to be scoring alcohol, going clubbing, and being in the know about the latest gossip—generally trying to act grown. A few of them were even having babies. None of them had long-term plans to secure a stable future and live independently; instead, they all talked about finding a good man to take care of them, getting married, and settling down. When I was with them, I spoke wistfully of the same things, but after my exposure to a different mindset, those sentiments became less sincere. I didn't fully recognize it at the time, but changing neighborhoods and high schools was my introduction to a new way of thinking, from settling for a stagnant, unsatisfactory life to pursuing one of ambition and unlimited potential and possibilities.

Mindset Shifts and Growth Transitioning to Adulthood Realities

This shift in mindset meant I had to overcome resistance and opposition to reach my highest potential as I transitioned from teenager to full-fledged adult. As we began our final semester senior year, my friend who was in my grade and graduating with me, informed me she had applied to a historically black college and university (HBCU), and I started thinking about what college I would apply to.

Despite buckling down in class, I was pretty much an average student in the C+ range, and I wasn't sure about my chances for acceptance. Even though my parents didn't pressure my brother and me about attending college, they wanted to make sure we learned skills so we could earn a better living than they had. I know if I wanted to attend an HBCU or another college, my parents would help me arrange financing for my tuition because my parents wanted us to have experiences they were unable to have.

After graduation I enrolled in the local community college to determine if college was for me. To my embarrassment I was required to take remedial courses in English and math. I thought the math classes were a joke because it was basic arithmetic, which I passed within the first two semesters before advancing to college math. But the remedial English classes opened my mind to the fundamentals of various writing styles I hadn't grasped in my earlier academic education because of distractions—both external and internal—that posed barriers to my learning. As I recognized my potential for learning, my mindset shifted, and I swiftly moved through the remedial courses, pushing past the stigma of having to take them while in college.

Even though I was doing well in community college, I still had challenges to face. After completing my third semester, I began working a full-time job at the post office to reduce my student loan obligation and to not burden my parents with taking care of me. So I was working a midnight shift then attending classes during the day, balancing a full load of four courses.

I also helped out at my dad's vending stand. I understood that was a family obligation; I didn't expect to be fully paid. I chose to work at the post office and not the family business because I wanted to be independent and earn my own money. Based on my experiences up to then, I considered myself a success and felt I was making it. I had graduated high school and was attending college. I would earn a degree, begin a career, save my money, and perhaps be able to buy a home right after I got married for my kids to grow up in. I'd be an honorable citizen who contributed positively to society. I thought if I stayed on the path and focused on my goals, I would beat the odds and fulfill my parents' dream of achieving more than they had, making them proud.

What I didn't factor in was the reality of life: biases, judgments, corruption, injustices. I was somewhat naïve in thinking the world was a fair place where everyone had good intentions. I had a wake-up call when I realized that was not the case, that despite my hard work to make good grades by studying, other students cheated or, it was rumored, slept with the professors. I also learned that it's not possible to do it all, i.e., carry a full course load, earn good grades, work full-time, and help out at the family business.

I also tried to maintain friendships with the girls I'd grown up with in my childhood school and old neighborhood, even though we had chosen different paths. It all became too much, and I suffered a nervous breakdown. My struggle for success had left me mentally and physically exhausted. At just nineteen years old, I learned the hard way that doing it all is a myth.

I didn't really process what had happened to me, but the counseling I received during my five days as an inpatient at a psychiatric facility helped me understand. I remember my mom and dad coming to get me and my mom praying over me after they brought me home. I also had difficulty accepting the fact that I needed to take medication to help control my moods and anxiety. I wanted to be normal like everyone else, to function without pills. And the medication made me gain weight, beginning a battle that went on for many months.

Faith to Faith: A Journey

After my release from the mental health facility, I had regular appointments at the clinic there for medication management reviews and follow-ups with a psychiatrist. I would get frustrated because the psychiatrist was not able to tell me when I would be able to stop taking the prescribed medication, saying "It's up to you to determine when that will be."

I had always been healthy and wasn't familiar with the concept of taking long-term medication. I thought of it being like an antibiotic: take it twice a day for ten days, and then you're done. I had not yet returned to school and had given up my job at the post office, so I settled into an empty daily routine of sleeping, eating, and watching TV. I slowly began to accept that I'd have to take the medication indefinitely. I also accepted that I might not ever finish college.

Then on one visit to the psychiatrist, I announced I was dissatisfied with doing so little, having so many follow-up appointments, and him not being able to tell me when I could stop taking the medication that was making me fat. The psychiatrist pointed out that the majority of my weight gain wasn't due to the pills but to inactivity, sitting around eating and watching TV. He suggested we end my regular visits and asked me to come back in three months, and I agreed.

A few weeks later I went with my mom to the local Walmart, where I encountered the two sisters I'd been friendly with in high school. We had lost contact after graduation. They couldn't conceal their surprise at the change in my appearance; I'd gained nearly one hundred pounds since they'd last seen me. I was still kind of out of it, and my mom told them I'd been ill. They invited me to have lunch with them the next day.

During our lunch they updated me about their lives. They both were working part-time and attending college, and one of them had a summer internship lined up at a good company, where she hoped to work full-time after earning her degree. As I listened to them, my mind shifted to the old days when we would discuss our goals and dreams for our lives after high school, and I became depressed because they were on track, and I'd fallen by the wayside.

The next day while lying in front the TV, I suddenly began sobbing uncontrollably, so much that I feared I was having another breakdown. I begged God for help, to allow me to function without my medication and confessed to Him that I was afraid I wouldn't be able to do it. I instantly felt a warmth spreading throughout my body. I didn't take my medication that day or any day since, and that was over twenty years ago. I believe that was the moment my spiritual chains were released. I began reflecting on the lunch with my old friends, remembering the goals I had set for myself after graduating. I started talking with God, asking Him how I could get back on track. I didn't want to live with my parents for the rest of their lives, but how could I live on $475 of monthly social security disability insurance benefits? Then the Holy Spirit started giving me instructions, directing me to contact the psychiatrist and ask him for help getting a job. A few days later I kept my appointment with the psychiatrist and asked him for resources in finding employment. I could see his eyes light up as if thinking: *She's finally got it,* and he handed me the business card of an employment specialist and told me to contact them.

I did contact that person, and we met a few days later. She connected me to the state's Vocational Rehabilitation Services, which paid the tuition for me to return to school. I became a student peer/mentor at the mental health clinic. After graduating with a bachelor's degree in rehabilitation services, I began working for the mental health clinic as an employment specialist.

My life was forever transformed when I experienced the power of God in a spiritual encounter. My faith increased, challenging me to see past my limitations and to trust God more with my life's journey. I learned how to surrender, to seek God's wisdom and understanding, to lay my will down, to discover what I wanted, and figure out how to make it happen. I prayed for God's direction and trusted His process, timing, and infinite wisdom.

I learned my life experiences had led me to a greater purpose: to serve humanity. I developed patience and greater compassion, especially for the most vulnerable among us. I created my brand, Caring with Compassion, as a call to action, promoting disability awareness, education, and compassion toward others. I create online education courses, training, workshops, digital content about disability awareness, and recently published my first e-book, *A Guide to Accessing Services and Resources in the Healthcare Social Services for Persons with Chronic Healthcare and Disabilities Quality of Life.* I also wrote the book *Caring with Compassion: A Legacy of Love,* honoring my parents' legacy. What a caregiver and healthcare professional has taught me about having a servant's heart, unconditional love, and compassion as I serve others.

I hope that by sharing my story and experiences, you are inspired and encouraged to live your best life on purpose, for purpose, in purpose.

Recognizing the need for having the right mindset moving forward to live your best life, here are three things I'd like you to consider on your journey.

Environmental change. A change in your environment can lead to significant changes that shift your mindset, allowing you to experience something different than what has become familiar and stagnant, hindering your growth. Evaluate your current environment on purpose.

Growth transitioning. As you evaluate and make changes in your environment, it will lead to transitions from the familiar to the unknown, and this is where you will recognize your growth for your purpose.

Faith to faith: A journey. Experiencing internal and external growth on the journey will challenge your faith as you move in your purpose you were created for.

About the Author

As a disability advocate, consultant, and educator, Ronita Boullt promotes disability awareness using thirty-plus years of experience in healthcare social services systems, supporting individuals with chronic healthcare conditions and disabilities. She educates many individuals with and without disabilities who need to understand how to navigate an integrated healthcare system by bringing awareness to healthcare professionals and medical providers in accessing services for consumers' quality of life, allowing individuals with disabilities to remain at home maximizing independence cost effectively.

Ronita hold a BS in rehabilitation services and counseling, she's a certified patient advocate and has worked as a case manager serving the most vulnerable populations: individuals with intellectual developmental disabilities, the elderly, disabled veterans, and those diagnosed with chronic health conditions.

Her most personal experiences have come from being a caregiver to her mom for fourteen years and her own health issues that placed her on the path of healthcare. Having navigated the healthcare systems for both herself and her mom, she has learned to use her voice to ensure that quality services are provided. She has advocated and worked in collaboration with various health care teams, maximizing appropriate services to accomplish rehabilitation, health goals, and quality care.

These personal experiences awakened her passion for educating the general population about disability awareness: how to serve persons with chronic health conditions and disabilities with more compassion, recognizing their abilities, taking a holistic person-centered planning approach, and becoming knowledgeable about appropriate resources to better serve them and maximize their independence and quality of life.

Please visit www.ronitaboullt.com to receive your Maximizing Independence for Quality of Life resource guide

Some chains that have kept you bound and enslaved are not your fault. Thay are your family history's fault. Now it's your responsibility to heal first, then break the cycle.

~Ari Squires

Daddy-Daughter Issues

Hurt. Broken. Confused. Angry. Frustrated. Disappointed. Resentful. Rejected.

These eight words sum up the emotions I held onto for over thirty years toward my biological father. Yet I decided to do what many hurt daughters would consider insane and chose to honor him. For you ladies who suffer from daddy-daughter issues, keep reading. This chapter will help you identify your truth through my personal truth in realizing it's not about the pain of what happened but the purpose of why it happened. By knowing my truth, I can own my dysfunctional experience as it was the very thing that unlocked my destiny.

To give you the landscape, my mother and father were high school sweethearts. They were together for twenty years, married for seventeen. Within that timeframe, my dad had five children of which I am the eldest daughter. Although he did live with us, I considered him present but absent. I witnessed my mom experience a lot of lonely nights crying. Eventually my mother had enough, and now they have been divorced for over twenty years.

From watching the hurt he caused my mother and not receiving the personal affection I was longing for, my desire to grow and foster a relationship with my dad faded. My naïve twelve-year-old-self thought the divorce would mean that now my sister and I would get two of everything, one from mom and one from dad. In my 20/20 hindsight vision, I realize how wrong it was to think that. I don't want to leave the impression he did nothing; however, I just wished he had done more. It bothered me to think that my dad was willing to watch my sister and me struggle financially. It just didn't seem fair to me that my mom was the only one who made sacrifices to take care of us.

Besides dealing with that as a youth, I was also broken. I always desired to be daddy's little girl, but after tattling on my dad to my mom that we were at another woman's house, I was cut off at four years old. I was on an everlasting quest for my dad to give me another chance to hang out with him and not tell. I worked so hard to be seen by him, but I received praises, kisses, and pats on the back from everyone but my dad. This broke me because although I had the attention of everyone else, it felt like I was seen by no one because the one person I wanted to see me did not. As his eldest daughter, I couldn't understand why he didn't see me the way others saw me: ambitious, charismatic, and diligent. I witnessed my mother's dedication, faithfulness, and tear-filled eyes only to realize that it wasn't just me he didn't see.

I was also confused that despite my efforts, I never heard him say: *Good job, Meisha. You made Daddy proud.* I worked hard to graduate in the top 5 percent of my class for middle school and high school. I went on to become the first in my family to graduate from college and study abroad in two different countries and afterward landed Fortune 100 corporate jobs. None of this appeared to be enough as it always came across as an expectation and not a congratulation.

All this together made me angry, frustrated, and disappointed to the point I thought I could just suppress the pain and move on without ever having to deal with it. Not dealing with it caused me to build so much resentment that when I did meet the love of my life, I struggled with not bringing that emotional baggage into the relationship.

Fast forward a couple of years. I met a man named Brian who changed my life. The reality is he was everything I had prayed for. When he proposed to me, my one stipulation was for us to attend premarital counseling. I knew the effect of not preparing for marriage, so in an effort to break the generational curse, I recognized we needed to start off building our foundation with God in the center of it. God was the one who designed marriage in the first place.

As we went through the premarital courses, our pastor asked me who was giving me away, and I said I didn't know yet. He looked surprised.

"Do you have a living father?"

I replied yes.

"Well, he should be giving you away."

Our pastor emphasized what the Bible said, which was to honor thy father and thy mother. Interestingly enough, the Bible does not list any exceptions, which means God expects us to do our part by honoring our parents.

This was a tough pill to swallow, and it got tougher when my fiancé told me I needed to have a talk with my dad prior to us getting married. He provided me with the hard truth that it was necessary to forgive my dad to avoid bringing the baggage of rejection into our marriage. He also went a step further and told me not to call him until I had spoken with my dad. Scared of the outcome but knowing how much I wanted us to be in the best position to have a strong marriage, I decided to write out my pain in a four-page letter to my dad. I will spare you the details of that letter, but just for a second imagine what you would say as a hurt, broken, confused, angry, frustrated, disappointed, resentful, rejected twenty-five-year-old girl.

As I approached the end of my expression, I felt somewhat relieved but nervous at the same time; I wasn't sure how he would take my truth. I pressed send and messaged my dad on his two-way pager to check his email. My heart pounded, and my hands trembled. Crazy thoughts were going through my head about what his reaction could be. Then the wait was over. He replied to my email saying he didn't know I felt that way and if I really didn't want him to give me away, then he wouldn't. But he would still pay his part for the wedding.

I felt bad because deep inside I did want my father to give me away, just not under the current circumstances. I recall getting so angry when he took credit for doing things he wasn't responsible for. We had each other's phone number and address, just not a true relationship. I did not want to walk down the aisle that way. After my father and I had a heart-to-heart conversation, I pushed the reset button and proudly accepted him to be the man to give me away.

If you are a father reading this, please note that your daughter needs your love and reassurance. You should be quick to ask for forgiveness and be willing to express things you may have dealt with growing up. She needs to hear your reasons for not being there.

On the day before my wedding and the entire day of my wedding, I was able to be daddy's little girl. I finally had his attention. I had forgiven my dad and was looking forward to a bright, lasting future with my husband.

My dysfunctional experience was the exact journey that propelled me into my destiny. My pain had purpose. In 2014 I opened a wedding planning and design company called Dream Celebrations, Inc. During wedding consultations I would ask the bride who was giving her away. Most times her response was the look of hurt I knew so well and could easily see she was a product of daddy-daughter issues.

Her body language would get tense with eye-rolling, a distorted facial expression, and head swirling as she would say, "I'm not letting my dad give me away. For what? He hasn't done anything for me."

I would then become a vessel, sharing experiences that brought me to my clarity point and in turn helping the bride to see the importance of honoring her father. I personally feel that the act of not honoring your father allows for generational curses to keep you chained to a reality that you do not have to take on.

After two years of working as a wedding planner, I realized so many couples were preparing for their one wedding day, but I didn't see the same effort and commitment preparing for their marriage. And without preparation, they could end up in a tough place costing them their marriage. I did some research and found that the national divorce rate is well over 50 percent, and it is at 70 percent for African-American couples. The role of father and the role of husband have some similarities, so if the bride does not respect or honor her father, she will find it difficult—whether consciously or unconsciously—to display that level of honor toward her husband. That leads to conflict and far too often, divorce.

It made me take a leap of faith to get aligned with my truth and rebrand myself because being a wedding planner wasn't my desire. It did not allow me the type of impact I was trying to achieve, which was helping women overcome within (WOW). I wanted to WOW my couples and their guests, not just through the beauty of planning, coordinating, and decorating but to show them the beauty of forgiveness and love. I settled on the title marriage planner and WOW expert. We help couples best prepare for their *marriage* all while transforming their venue into a magical space that makes them and their guests say, WOW! when their room is revealed.

Our couples complete an assessment that identifies their strengths and growth areas. We then pair them with a licensed professional counselor to help them develop in the areas of communication, conflict resolution, financial management, affection and sexuality, and relationship roles to name a few. We understand issues come up and differences occur; therefore, we just want to make sure our couples have the tools to help them sustain their marriages.

You may be thinking: *Okay, happy ending,* but I can't leave you thinking that the struggle of forgiveness is easy. Years have gone by since the original conversation with my dad where I thought I had totally forgiven him. Within the past few years, I've noticed that some of those old feelings had reemerged. I didn't know or couldn't understand how that could happen after I had forgiven him. By then I knew my soul's purpose was to help brides forgive their dads so they could fully love their husbands. However, knowing I still struggled with the relationship between myself and my dad, made me feel like a hypocrite, so I shied away from my calling. I stopped telling couples about the special, unique service our company was offering.

I took a different approach. I decided to pray to understand why those feelings were recurring so I could really help brides fully forgive their dads. Once you forgive someone that should settle it. But those eight words kept coming back to me when I thought about my dad. I had to get honest and assess why it was so hard to simply let go. People tell you to do this all the time, but I haven't heard anyone tell us how to let go. After undergoing my own healing process, I was able to dissect the how-to into a five-step healing program with an emphasis on showing hurt people how to LETGO, so they can live their best life. I especially teach this to brides because I want what God wants for their union, which is for it to prosper.

Carrying unforgiveness was my chain that needed to be broken. I used to feel like I was hurting my dad by not forgiving him because I wanted him to feel the same pain and rejection I felt. But unforgiveness only causes grief and additional hurt. It allows you to continually relive and replay all that happened, and then you get stuck there. I caught myself saying it is hard to forgive but American gospel singer and Grammy award winner Tina Campbell elevated my perspective with, "It's too hard not to."

People need to understand it's the weight you can't see that causes you not to soar in various areas of your life. Think about it; planes have weight requirements. If the luggage or the passengers weigh too much, the plane will not take off. Something or someone will have to be removed. That's how it is in life. If we walk around with too much baggage, we will be weighted down and not able to soar.

My weight represented bitterness and unforgiveness. Once I was finally able to LETGO, I became free. I began not looking at myself as a victim. So many people tell you: *Things happen for a reason.* You've possibly even told someone that yourself. But when it applies to your own life, it's a harder pill to swallow. I've had to learn to embrace my journey, my trials, and tribulations because things really *do* happen for a reason.

Because of the pain and hurt I've gone through, I now help women forgive their fathers faster than the thirty years it took me. I help impact the lives of women, their marriages, and families. We go through things so that we can be a blessing to others and meet them where they are and not judge them. I am helping to reduce the divorce rate and putting couples in the best position to have a strong marriage. I am breaking generational curses and helping women see the value and importance of protecting their marriages and families.

Even though I did not have the type of relationship I thought was ideal with my earthly father, I've been able to have that plus so much more with my Heavenly Father. God makes me think I am his most precious daughter. No offense to anyone reading this, but I am Daddy's little girl. He provides for me during times of lack. He gives me shortcuts and shows me favor. He is always present. He gives me money, sometimes even in the form of an anonymous check. He even gave me a car. I am totally spoiled by Him.

I want readers to know God is real, and you can have a real relationship with Him. You can be Daddy's little girl too, even if you weren't that with your earthly father. But you have to LETGO of those eight negative adjectives. Oddly enough, eight represents a new beginning and the start of a new era. This is your time to take back control of your life. There are thousands of people who are not being helped by you because you are weighted down.

Isaiah 61:7 (NIV) says: "Instead of your shame you will receive a double portion, and instead of disgrace you will rejoice in your inheritance. And so you will inherit a double portion in your land, and everlasting joy will be yours."

I interpret this to mean we will receive double for our trouble. Then why must we hold so many grudges and ill-will toward the person who caused us grief? Have you ever considered that person might have been used to allow you to unlock your purpose? Did it occur to you that person may have done the best job they knew how to do at the time? When we think about parenthood, we must take notice that it doesn't come with a book, and the baby isn't born with a manual. Did you ever stop to consider how that person was raised, what life experiences caused them to act the way they do? No, most times we do not. I know I didn't. I was so focused on me and what happened to me that I never considered thinking about him and the generational curses he was dealing with.

Hopefully you see how honoring my father after the pain and through purpose wasn't insane. But it is insane for you to not LETGO, so let's stop the insane behavior and start doing what will change generations. There is a legacy inside of you. Let's reveal it to the world.

About the Author

Tameishia Pigford, affectionately known as Meisha, is a certified wedding planner and event designer who creates over-the-top, premium experiences for her clients that leave them saying wow! After working in human resources where she developed her people skills and helped organize corporate events, Meisha designed her own wedding, sparking her love of event planning.

Meisha now owns an award-winning planning and design firm, Dream Celebrations, Inc., and through her work as a marriage planner and WOW expert, she assists couples with not only preparing for their big day but also for their marriage. Her goal is to help lower the divorce rate in this country one couple at a time.

**Please Visit http://letgothepast.com
to receive your Daddy-Daughter Forgiveness audio**

Chasing a Ghost

I was a young boy between the age of five and seven years old when I last saw my father. I remember being so ecstatic spending time with him. He gave me $20, bought me a brand-new JanSport backpack, and got me a kid's cheeseburger meal to go at Burger King. My last memory of him was telling me to sit at the bus stop and wait for him to come back.

In my young mind I figured he just had a quick errand to run and would surely be back to get me. Hours passed, and I sat, swinging my feet, patiently awaiting his return. Finally a woman came up to me and asked why I was sitting at the bus stop all alone. She somehow contacted my mother, and I was taken home. Looking back, it was then that my childhood resentment morphed into hatred for the man I called my father.

My mother told me many stories about my dad that often made me feel worthless. She told me that my father did not want me because he was too young to be a father. She told me that he actively encouraged her to abort me, or he would leave. I am of course thankful to my mother for keeping and caring for me until adulthood.

However, like many children with an absentee parent, I held a high level of resentment toward my mother and father. I've heard many stories of how children were angry at their mothers because they just knew that there was something that she did to make the father leave. We often believe that the absent parent is perfect and can do no wrong. Though it's difficult to admit, I felt that way for a long time. After all the hurtful things about my father were relayed to me, I found myself becoming emotionless, and my heart was as cold as an icebox.

Though I could not stand my father, my mother wanted me to have a relationship with his side of the family. She would take me over to my paternal grandma's house, and all my aunts and uncles would be there. My favorites were Auntie Bonnie, Auntie Faye, and Uncle Fly, who always gave me money and ensured that I was taken care of.

During one visit to my grandmother's house, I was greeted by my Uncle Fly, who was on the porch with all these half-naked women. As a child I could not understand why so many women were hanging out at my grandmother's house and how my uncle seemed to have control over all of them. He would point to each woman and direct her to do some task—*You, you, and you, go to the store; you go cook me some food, etc.*

I asked him, "Are these all your girlfriends?"

To which he replied, "Yeah, they all love me and will do whatever I tell them to do."

I looked at Uncle Fly as somewhat of a father figure. From that point on I figured that was the way of life: for a man to have multiple women to fulfill all sexual requests and have all of them love you unconditionally with zero drama. To this day I think my Uncle Fly was a pimp, but I cannot confirm or deny. During my early teenage years, I did not believe in relationships, but I wanted to have sex. Like most boys who are raised without a positive father in the home, I got most of my sex education from my boys in the streets. My mother sat down with me and gave a quick and generalized lecture about sex, which went in one ear and out the other. I never had a man give me a mature and detailed conversation about sex, namely the consequences of having unprotected sex. As a result I became a father at fifteen.

I was in denial at first and refused to believe that I was a having a child. Over time I came to accept it and followed my mother's advice on looking for jobs to provide for my baby. Those jobs did not pay enough, and I felt I was working more than spending time with my child. Working a nine to five was not feasible, so I began to get more involved with the streets. I idolized basketball players and drug dealers. I looked at the basketball players as what I wanted to be in the distant future. I viewed the drug dealers as role models/father figures in the here and now because like many young men in the hood, I saw the fast money with little effort.

I was so fascinated by the fast life and making easy money that I began selling drugs for the big-time drug dealers in my neighborhood. Selling drugs for them was my way of giving back to them for teaching me life lessons, buying new school clothes, and shielding me from harm in the streets like a father would have done. They tried to keep me in line and always told me to stay my a** in school, stop skipping class, and to make a difference in the world one day by doing more good than bad.

Later I became affiliated with the Gangster Disciples and began learning from the old heads we called original gangsters. These guys were well-respected in the neighborhood and had done everything from drug dealing to murder. They instantly took me under their wing because I was in the streets more than I was at home. During my junior year of high school, I was shot two times and nearly died from my wounds and severe blood loss. I went through several months of rehab and almost lost my leg to infection. The doctor told me that I might never be able to have more kids because the bullet had ruptured veins close to my private area. I went through months of depression and became enraged. I went from feeling like a victim and turned into a perpetrator. I felt like Tupac; it was *me against the world.* After about six months of therapy, I went back to selling drugs and gangbanging like the tragic event never even happened, and I was crazier than ever.

It was times like that when I truly longed for my biological father. As a father myself I could never fathom abandoning my children. I cannot imagine missing all the milestones and achievements. Over the years I have found myself attempting to "earn" his love, something no child should have to do. Much of my motivation and drive to be great was to gain his approval. I have spent many years thinking if only I could achieve this or accomplish that my father would surely be proud of me and want to be in my life. It's been forty-four years, and that day has not come.

I have moments where I think that maybe he was never taught how to be a father and that this is a generational chain I believe I am finally breaking. Like many in the black community, I unfortunately do not know much about my family history beyond my parents' generation. I knew my grandmother, but never heard anything about my grandfather.

I gave up on ever having a relationship with him though that has always been my strongest desire. When I turned forty, with my mother's and paternal aunt's encouragement, I attempted to connect with him. I spoke with him on the phone, and we decided that it would be good for me to visit him. I bought the plane ticket, bought gifts for him, told all my family and friends. I was beyond thrilled to finally be face-to-face with my dad again; I just knew that once he got to know me, he would love me! But unfortunately, just like many times before, he stood me up. This moment took me right back to that day at the bus stop; I felt alone, afraid, angry, and embarrassed.

So as one would expect, this is still a chain that has kept me stagnant. I find it difficult to trust people, and I still battle with abandonment issues. In personal relationships I find myself never fully committing. I never want to lose control and give my all to anyone for fear of being discarded. One good thing that came out of this experience with my father is that I have learned what I do not want to be. I have vowed never to make my children feel unloved. I take pride in being there for my children, through the good and the bad.

I have released putting the responsibility for my father leaving on my mother. For a long time I believed that my mom did something to cause my father to abandon me. She raised me to be the man I am today. The pain from not having my father around made me act out a lot as a child and continually disobey my mother. I finally realized the reason I did this was because I was mad at her for not convincing him to stay. As a man he made the decision to leave, not my mother. My father holds total responsibility for walking out my life as a child.

For me, *it's time for change* means releasing the hurt and moving on, living life without regrets. I must make peace with knowing that I may never have the relationship with my father that I have always desired. I must live my life to the fullest and not allow anything to hold me back. It means using my experience to mentor other young men with absentee fathers and giving them the coaching and guidance that we as black men so desperately need.

I realized it was time for a change in November 1995 when my mom kicked me out of the house. Chicago police officers raided our home because they suspected drugs were on the premises. They broke down the back door and came into the house with guns drawn. They found nothing, but I was forcibly removed because of disorderly conduct. My mom told the police officers that I could never come back to her home again and if I did she wanted me arrested. I was now homeless, in the middle of a Chicago winter with nowhere to go. The streets became my new home. I slept on the trains during the night and caught a few hours of rest at my friend's house during the day. That's when I learned the real value of a dollar and ate breakfast, lunch, and dinner off $10 a day. Now a new chain was created; I did not just have hatred for my father, I had an extreme dislike for my mother as well.

Three months later God finally answered my prayers, and I was accepted into the United States Air Force. My mother had no knowledge that I had joined the military, and I knew she would blow a gasket when she found out. I called her three months later after boot camp and told her I had joined. She instantly hung up on me. Before I knew it months had passed without us talking, and now I was leaving the States and off to Germany for four years.

During my military tour in Germany, I began to mature more after the birth of my second child. I was still struggling with showing any kind of emotion or getting totally committed to a relationship. Those emotional chains were still pulling me down even as an adult. Seven years later I got married and had my third child. I wanted to do things differently this time around and not have any more kids out of wedlock. In the military I never really had the opportunity to raise my previous children, so I wanted to make sure I did this time. I always tell my kids they have three different daddies, and they look crazy at me. I explain to them I was at three different points in my life when they were born. Loving and caring for my children helped in my healing process from growing up as a fatherless child. I was learning how to love unconditionally by pouring all my love into children and getting it all back in return.

Learning how to love others no matter how you might have been treated helped me to love harder. I can willingly express my emotions more now. Since releasing the pain of the past, I have become a better man and father to my children. I have learned from my past experiences how to take a negative situation and turn it around into something positive.

Despite years of trauma and difficulties, I am proud of the man I am and the man I am becoming. I have accomplished so much more than anyone ever expected, and you can too. I have defied the odds and broken many chains in my life. Today I can say that I'm a God-fearing man, retired military veteran, excellent father, business owner, and community leader. I'm a man who lives life to the fullest and strives to be better every day while giving back to the youth in my community. I found out a few years ago that my father was an entrepreneur as well. I had always wondered where the desire to own my business originated. It was already in my blood. As much as I never wanted to be like that man, we shared the passion of being our own boss.

My greatest hope is to one day finally have a healthy relationship with my biological father. I have spent so many years chasing the idea of having a relationship with him that it changed me as a man. I have always worked through whatever shortfalls or obstacles that came my way to prove something to him. I wanted him to know that he made a mistake walking out of my life as a child. The pain I felt of not being wanted by my father, carried on in adulthood and affected every relationship whether professional or personal.

I appreciate my father for providing me with a blueprint on how to not to be as a dad. I have broken the generational chain. My kids receive everything from me a father should provide because I know what I missed as a child. Once I released those chains of feeling never being good enough to be loved, it enabled me to express my love more freely. I have finally found inner peace with the situation that had me chained down my entire life. Even if I never get the opportunity to have a relationship with my father, I will continue to love others and take what I have learned to grow more as a man.

I hope my story and experiences can be useful to someone else. It took the OGs in the neighborhood to tell me old stories about what they had been through when they were young to guide me to do better. My story and the stories of others can be useful in preventing you from making the same mistakes, and you can be a better man.

My purpose in life is to love my children unconditionally and pay forward to someone else the information that helped me. I feel I have been through the fire but still made it through by the grace of God and a praying mother.

Here are a few tips I can give you that can be useful for your personal and professional success:

First, always be honest because people will respect you more and want to do business with you. Be respectful of others' time, money, and ideas.

Second, have a *never give up* attitude. Always believe in yourself even when others do not. You can be your own worst enemy in your personal life and professional career. My struggles and setbacks in life could have defeated me. I have always believed that the sun comes after the storm, and I knew one day I would make it through. Never give up on yourself, and keep pressing through no matter the disadvantages against you. Defy the odds and become successful.

Third, release all chains and allow nothing to hold you back from chasing your destiny and fulfilling your dreams. Always keep in mind that there are people in far worse situations than you who have overcome their obstacles. Everything starts with believing in yourself and waking up every morning with a purpose to do something great in life. Break whatever chains might hold you back—whether physical, emotional, or spiritual—and embrace the opportunity to live free.

A favorite quote of mine comes from the rapper Drake. He said, "Never let success get to your head, and never let failure get to your heart."

Don't forget the people who assisted you along the way. There are several individuals I know who've had great success in life but never give back. People are drawn to a person that is genuine, trustworthy, and unwilling to let success change them in a negative manner. You cannot let failure be the reason you give up and never try again.

About the Author

Rondale Alexander, who grew up on the South Side of Chicago, Illinois, is the CEO of Rondavu, LLC. During his six-year tenure, Rondale has overseen operations and strategic planning for Rondavu Talent Management, which represents several celebrity clients. He has helped shape his clients' careers and guided them toward new opportunities. He has set up public appearances, offered advice on contract negotiation, and helped to build his clients' overall brand.

Prior to this role, Rondale spent twenty years in the United States Air Force, with deployments including Qatar, South Korea, and Kosovo. Before retiring with an honorable discharge, Rondale rescued two men from a major car accident, rendering immediate first-aid that helped save their lives. For his act of heroism, Rondale received Air Force-wide recognition.

Rondale holds a BA in organizational management and is currently pursuing an MBA at the University of the Incarnate Word in San Antonio, Texas. In his spare time Rondale enjoys traveling, caring for his children, and mentoring at-risk youth.

Please visit http://bit.ly/Rondavu7MajorPitfallsToAvoid to receive your guide on 7 Major PitfallstoAvoid While Trying to Pursue Your Talent

When Love Hurts

I was born into a family that did not know how to express love and with a generational curse of domestic violence. The odds were stacked against me from the time I left my mother's womb.

As far back as I can remember, I was always looking for love from men and things. When I say *things* I mean clothes. Shopping made me feel good. When I was sixteen my mother took me down to the health clinic to get birth control pills. She didn't talk about it to me; she didn't explain why she was doing it or anything about sex. My mother was mean and strict. We couldn't hang out or do things like normal teenagers, which is why I couldn't understand why she put me on the pill in the first place.

That was right around the time my mother and father split, which didn't affect me at all because my father was never around. He was an alcoholic, and my mother never really seemed to care. My parents never displayed love for us. I knew this was not a regular home; it always seemed cold, broken, and depressing. I just wanted to get out of there. I expected more from my parents. I wanted to be held and told that they loved me. I wanted them to take us places and do things that other families did. I wanted to be encouraged or for one of them to help me with my homework. I expected them to act like they cared for the children they brought into this world.

I would not say that I was a bad teenager growing up. I did sneak out some and talk back, but I didn't think I did anything so bad to be beaten with wooden sticks, brooms, and extension cords, but that was her form of discipline.

After my father left my mom got a boyfriend. That was the first time I was exposed to domestic violence, but back then I didn't know what it was. My mom's boyfriend would beat her then tell her that he loved her. The more this happened it planted a picture in my mind that a man can show his affection and love by beating you. This same boyfriend came into our room and tried to touch us. When I told my mom, she didn't believe me. It took a neighbor that I shared the information with to convince her I was telling the truth. She kicked him out afterward.

I was about seventeen years old when I shared with a guidance counselor at school about the abuse I was receiving at home. She told me about the emancipation process: you could file papers with the juvenile court stating why you wanted to divorce your parents and if they agreed, all they had to do was sign a document, and you were free to leave and would no longer be under their supervision.

Emancipation could set me free from the house of hell, so I took the necessary steps. The day I was preparing to leave my heart ripped apart as I packed. I imagined my mother would come over and ask: *Why are you leaving?* But she didn't, and my thought was: *Why isn't she trying to stop me? She must not love me. If she did love me, she wouldn't let me leave. She doesn't care about me.*

I left, and we didn't speak for about a year. I went to stay with a friend and eventually at nineteen got my own apartment, setting in motion a chain of events that would alter my life forever. I left home broken, unloved, and unwanted, when all I really wanted was my parents to love me. But how could they? They didn't understand emotions.

My search for love took off with a bang. I started looking for love in all the wrong places. I was living the fast life of clubbing, drinking, and doing things I had no business doing. One of my best friends was seeing a guy who was friends with her cousin. She told me her cousin wanted to meet me. He had come by my job a couple of times, and we all decided to watch a movie at my place. I was kind of hesitant because I had heard he was a drug dealer. But I was a little naïve and trusted my best friend.

Movie night came, and we were all sitting in my living room, which was dark except for the light from the television. I was on one side of the living room with my date, and my best friend was on the other side. As we sat and watched the movie my date began to whisper in my ear: *Let's go into the bedroom.* He did that on and on, and I continued to say no. Even though I was sleeping with men, I didn't sleep with anyone on the first date or let them into my bedroom.

He became frustrated and grabbed a chunk of my hair in the middle of my head and pulled it hard. The pain I felt was unexplainable. He did this very discretely and insisted that I go to the bedroom, or he would pull my hair out. I convinced myself: *Cathy, just go with him to the room, he just wants to talk and chill.*

As we walked into the room, he still had a grip on my hair. He shut the door and motioned me to the bed still gripping my hair. He put me on the bed and got on top of me and whispered in my ear that if I screamed or said anything, he would kill me. I had no reason to not take him seriously because he was a drug dealer, and I truly believed he would kill me. As he tried to penetrate me, I begged him to not do it. He pulled my hair with one hand and forced himself inside of me with the other.

While I was sexually assaulted, I did not fight back or try to flee. My body froze, and I was paralyzed in a state of incredible fear. I asked God: *Why are you letting this happen? Why don't you love me? Please make him stop.*

Once he was done he reminded me of what he would do if I said anything. We walked out of the room as if nothing had happened. I would remain silent for years before sharing it with my best friend and many more years before I would break my silence and share it with the world. I felt guilty and ashamed because I didn't fight back. I was afraid that people would blame me for what happened. The burden at times was overwhelming. I went from being a talkative person to having a flat affect, quiet, reserved, and I had difficulties expressing myself.

The rape, my broken home, childhood abuse, being unloved, not loving myself, not knowing my worth, low self-esteem, and years of physical, mental, verbal, and psychological abuse, at the hands of different men held me captive in chains. Wallowing in the pain made me unable to forgive and love someone else. I didn't trust anyone, and if I could not get what I was looking for out of one man, I would move to the next. It was like I was looking for my next fix. There were times when all I could do was to sit, cry, and try to survive. Even with all the people I knew, I still felt alone. I felt as if my life didn't matter. There was even a time when I thought about killing myself. It was just a thought, no plan of how.

One-day God spoke to me through all this pain. He had not deserted me, and He did love me. He showed me that He did care about everything that was happening to me and that there was purpose in my pain. God never wastes hurt. He showed me what love is in scripture. I would read 1 Corinthians 13:4–8 every day.

> Love is patient, love is kind. It does not envy, it does not boast, it is not proud. It does not dishonor others, it is not self-seeking, it is not easily angered, it keeps no record of wrongs. Love does not delight in evil but rejoices with the truth. It always protects, always trusts, always hopes, always perseveres. Love never fails.

Prayer and strengthening my relationship with Him help me see that I really did have a life to live. I started seeing things I didn't know were in me. I woke up one day and got all my hair cut off and a tattoo. My friends thought I was crazy. But I was a changed woman. After I got more into scripture, I found out that tattooing the body was wrong as a Christian, so I said I would never get another tattoo. Reading scripture also showed me that I was beautifully and wonderfully made. It showed me that I was not the names I was called like ugly and fat. God showed me that He wanted me to help other people going through that same hurt. He wanted me to share my story. He used all the pain and gave me the gift of speaking to be able to help others. He embraced me and showed me how to embrace myself. Reading scripture, prayer, and meditation got me through and still gets me through. In order for me to embrace my journey, I had to do it unbothered by what people would think about me being raped and abused. All the pain I experienced had to happen to bring me healing and to prevent greater suffering.

I needed healing and closure, or I would remain lost and unfulfilled my whole life. I didn't want that. I felt there must be more out there for me than depression and lack. I realized that the first step in my healing transformation was learning how to love myself. This process would not be easy. There were things I had done and said that I was ashamed of. One of the hardest things I had to let go of was thinking that no one would want me if they knew I had been raped. This was one of the reasons I stayed silent for so long. The embarrassment was eating away inside of me.

For me to start loving me, I first had to forgive myself for all the wrong I had done in the past. That meant I had to walk in my truth. I had to accept me for who I was and allow God to come into my heart and help me be fully transparent. Then I had to forgive those who I thought played a part in hurting me. That wasn't easy for me, but forgiveness is not for others; forgiveness is for you. It set me free from feeling like they held me hostage.

I forgave my parents because I think they did their best with what they had. I am not making excuses for what my parents did. I am not saying that they couldn't have done things differently. The abuse was a generational curse. My great grandmother was abused, my grandmother, my mom, and aunts. My mom abusing me was a choice, but she might not have realized what she was doing was wrong. Because she wasn't loved she did not know how to love me. I realized later that I could not fix my parents. But I could show them how to love, and I did just that. I started telling them that I loved them. I would hug and embrace them, call them, take them places, and do family things. I had to rewrite my story so that they and my child could see something different. It was up to me to break the generational curse and chains that held me and my family back for far too many years and show them something different.

If we just keep sweeping our chains under the rug, more children will be hurt. We will never get to a better place. The cycle will never end. If the cycle continues, we remain lost, broken, and never become free.

Seeing my mom get abused by her boyfriends, sent me into the world thinking that if a man hit you, he loved you. Therefore I allowed this to happen in my relationships. My biggest challenge was asking myself why? Why did I allow these things to happen? What was it about me? The search deep inside would be another life-changing realization.

When you make the decision to start loving yourself, you won't allow anyone to treat you badly or put you in an uncomfortable situation. One of my favorite Bible verses that I read every day while healing was Psalm 139:14: "I praise you because I am fearfully and wonderfully made; your works are wonderful, I know that full well." God helped me realize there was nothing wrong with me and that He made me in His image. I learned what true love was by loving myself. I also learned I could accept and give the right kind of love.

Experiencing any kind of trauma can affect you for years and destroy your life if you let it. It happens to too many of us. That's why the *no more chains* movement is so needed. When it comes to domestic violence and sexual assault, know that it's not your fault. You can't blame yourself.

In addition to forgiveness and self-love, there is a process you must go through anytime the devil comes after you. First, realize exactly who the enemy is. Our battle is spiritual. The devil will use people and your past to make you think badly about yourself. Negative self-talk is high on the devil's list for seeking and destroying who God says you are. The devil is a liar. Don't believe anything that he tells you negative about yourself. Don't allow him to let your past destroy you.

I have helped so many people by sharing about my sexual assault and domestic violence. Using my voice landed me a chance to go before millions on national television. I learned that it is okay to speak up and speak out.

Second, replace any lie you're told with the truth. Silence everything in your mind that is negative or hurtful and says that you are not enough. No matter what you are going through, God loves you and will help you turn pain into gain. Everyone has a past and goes through something. We cannot let our past define us.

I was supposed to be a statistic. I wasn't supposed to survive what had happened to me. But I chose to not allow it to destroy me. It's hard to overcome being raped because of the trauma associated with it, but with God's help I did it. The childhood abuse I suffered could have very well sent me in the direction of violence and crime. I could have let low self-esteem, feeling unworthy, and hopelessness from being abused in my adult years take a toll on the rest of my development. There are so many little girls who grow into adult women walking around hurting. I could have been one of those women. I chose to do something about it. You can too. I believe if we acknowledge the problem and seek help, there is healing and hope.

Realizing my self-worth saved my life, and it can do the same for you no matter where you are in your journey to healing. Understand that our self-worth should never depend on others. Yes, compliments and appreciation are nice and powerful, but accepting yourself and your own uniqueness is liberating. When you love yourself, there is no need to pretend or wish you were someone else.

Learning to love myself allowed me to celebrate the woman that God created, and it helped me live out my primary purpose. Think about how your restoration can help change your family dynamics. Removing your mask of *I'm not hurting* allows for the authentic person to come out. Doing this will take some time. Peeling back the layers of lies the enemy told you to define yourself by won't be easy. In doing this realize what is unique about you and celebrate your uniqueness. Remember you are not like anyone else. He set you apart.

I have learned to live my life unapologetically. Learn to be okay with saying no, set boundaries, and balance family and work. Your journey will also require you to regularly examine your circle of influence. Not having the right people in your circle could hurt your journey to self-love. On your journey to self-love, it is important to stay in your lane. Know the role you play. Yield to God; not everything will go your way.

Unconditional love is another step on the journey to self-love. Learning to love people unconditionally is a commitment. Loving someone unconditionally does not mean that we must agree with them; it means we accept them as they are in their growth. That was hard for me. What helped me was thinking about how Christ loves me unconditionally despite the things I've done.

God used my story for His glory. In my healing and transformation, I realized that I did not want anyone else to go through what I had. In praying for a way to help, God gave me a vision for the nonprofit MyHelpMyHope Foundation, which brings awareness to domestic violence, sexual assault, and human sex trafficking. My organization helps women and their children fleeing these types of trauma situations. We provide resources, education, training, goal coaching, shelter, food, school uniforms, and Christmas for children in local domestic violence and homeless shelters. We believe that everyone has the right to a healthy relationship.

As an advocate for these causes, I discovered my gift for speaking and helping those affected by these traumas to heal and walk in their purpose. I do not heal anyone. God heals. He uses me to help. I have written self-help books, I speak, and I have started a life coaching consulting business to help those who are hurting and having a hard time to push past their pain. I consider myself a stepping stone as one journeys to self-discovery. I have a gift to help people learn how beautiful and wonderful they are by teaching them how to love themselves inside and out.

Self-love is what breaks generational chains. Learning how to love myself changed my life. I learned to focus on the things I was doing right instead of obsessing over the things I was doing wrong. I learned to focus on all the great things about me instead of on what I didn't like about myself. Self-love is not being selfish. Self-love is necessary for your journey. Learning to love yourself leads to happiness. You light up the world with your gifts, and you inspire others to do the same. We cannot love anyone else or give love until we first learn to love ourselves. Self-love means growing and making healthier choices. One outlet I used was journaling my feelings and emotions. This will help you learn what is working for you and what is not working for you. Ask for help. It is okay to do this. We cannot do everything by ourselves.

God is love, and love starts at home. Displaying love to our children creates healthy relationships, healthy families, healthy communities, and a healthy world. When we learn the art of self-love, we create a world full of happiness and joy and release ourselves from emotional heartache and pain.

My journey to self-love has baffled many. People wonder how I got through all the pain, the abuse, sexual assault, church hurt, and so much more. They wonder how I went from hating high school with low grades because I was bullied, to graduating with three bachelor's degrees at one time, founding a nonprofit, and starting my own business. I decided that enough was enough. I wanted something different out of my life. After all I went through, God had to have a purpose for my life. On my journey to self-love, I found out how strong I was. I discovered I was smart, intelligent, resilient, beautiful, empowering, inspiring, a leader, a teacher, a winner, and people needed what I had to offer. Self-love will give you peace and freedom.

Nothing can hold you back when you love yourself. Step into your greatness. Be yourself and let your light shine in the world. I thank God for redemption and deliverance. I am no longer ashamed.

> *God whispers to us in our pleasures, speaks in our conscience, but shouts in our pains.*
> —C.S. Lewis

About the Author

Cathy Staton brings with her over twenty years of leadership development experience as a self-published author, Christian counselor, motivational speaker, philanthropist, and life and business coach. Cathy has received leadership training from dynamic coaches such as Latrece Williams McKnight and Ari Squires. Her cutting-edge life skill strategies and uncompromising integrity are the hallmarks of her services to help women find their voice and use life's stumbling blocks to rebuild their lives.

Cathy serves as a domestic violence and sexual assault advocate providing a message of hope, encouragement, empowerment and inspiration. She is the founder of MyHelpMyHope Foundation, a 501(c)(3) nonprofit organization that assists women and children in crisis situations. She is also the CEO of Cathy Staton Coaching & Consulting, a company that provides affordable life coaching to those who want to reach their maximum potential in life and business. Through one-on-one coaching, group coaching, and custom presentations, she uses proven techniques to help people find fulfillment doing what they love.

Cathy is the recipient of numerous awards including the Wavy TV Channel 10 Who Care award, the Zeta Phi Beta Sorority Finer Woman award, Hampton Roads Gazeti Exemplar award, ACHI Magazine Woman of the Year award, ACHI Magazine Philanthropist award, Genieve Shelter Hero award, and the Garden of Hope Unity award from Gethsemane Community Fellowship Church. Cathy's work has been featured on the nationally syndicated Dr. Oz Show, Wavy 10 News, 13 News Now, and WTKR Channel 3. Cathy has also been featured in publications such as the Virginian-Pilot, the New Journal and Guide, the Hampton Roads Gazeti, and Tidewater Women. In 2017 the Obama Administration, Michelle Obama, and Oprah Winfrey selected The MyHelpMyHope Foundation as a change maker. Cathy has earned an AS in psychology, a BS in Christian counseling, a BS in life coaching, a BS in addiction and recovery from Liberty University, and is currently earning her Master's Degree in Professional Counseling.

Please visit www.cathystatonfreebie.com to receive your Rewrite Your Story step-by-step action guide

A Product of the Projects

My early childhood was spent growing up in the Butler Housing Project in Fort Worth, Texas, where my brother and I were raised by our mother and grandmother. Nineteen years old and single, my mother had to drop out of school and stop attending church because she was an unwed mother. However, my grandmother made sure we attended church regularly which seemed like every day. I learned how to read by reading Bible scriptures. My mother constantly stressed the importance of an education, so I have always excelled academically. Then my mother met someone that would change our lives forever.

Prior to meeting *him*, my mother always took us with her wherever she went. No matter if it was to the store, to a friend's house, or to the park where she spent time with her friends, we were right there with her. The three of us were inseparable. Shortly after my mother introduced us to *him*, the four of us moved out of the projects, taking me and my brother away from a home filled with so much love and affection. Instead we found ourselves in a place where we felt isolated and alone. If she wasn't yelling at us, she was ignoring us. We couldn't talk to her like we used to. She would wake us up to go to school, feed us dinner, then we went to bed. If we asked her for help with our homework, she would yell, "Go figure it out!"

I remember when *he* lost his job after getting hurt on a construction site. We felt like servants getting his beer and cigarettes, attending to his every need. Worst of all he would tell my mother to beat us. When we lived with my grandmother, my mother didn't hit us if we did something wrong. She would talk to us and explain why we shouldn't do what we did. Now she had turned into a strict disciplinarian. We received beatings all the time, even though we usually did not deserve them. If she was having a bad day, she would beat us. If she was mad at *him*, she would beat us.

My brother received a beating I'll never forget. *He* told my mother to beat my brother with an extension cord, and she did. At one point my brother accidentally hit her while grabbing for the cord. My mother started pounding him with her fist, fighting like he was a man. My brother was bleeding and screaming. I jumped in between them, pushing my mother away from him. When she tried to hit me, I ran outside to the pay phone and called my grandmother, who came to get us. My mother was crying as we packed up our things. She told us if we left, not to come back. My brother and I were crying. We didn't want to leave our mother, but we didn't like the way she treated us either.

For more than a year, we lived in the Butler Housing Projects with my grandmother in her one-bedroom apartment. I slept on a piece of foam on a foldout bed behind her bedroom door, and my brother slept on the floor in the living room. My mother never called. I was angry at her for treating us that way. She had changed because of him.

Although I remained on the honor roll at school, my attitude was terrible. I was so angry with my mother, and I took it out on others. For example, if someone at school was being picked on, I would speak up for them. Most of the time it turned into fights. That day I was forced to protect my brother from my mother had changed me. I took on the role of protector and defender. If someone said something I didn't like, I would fight back verbally or physically. That was the total opposite of how my grandmother raised me.

Words can't harm you.

Don't let people control you.

You can't control what others do to you, but you can control your response to it.

My mind was so messed up I ignored her loving words and great wisdom. I mean, what else was I supposed to do? I was hurting. My mom, the first woman I'd ever loved, gave up on me for some man and left me to grow up without a mom.

Eventually my grandmother could no longer afford to take care of us on her fixed income, so we had to move back in with my mother. She didn't talk to us, just at us. She totally isolated herself from us. We had to talk to her through her closed bedroom door.

We didn't eat dinner together. She would feed us then she ate dinner with him. We couldn't get seconds, so if my brother was still hungry, I would give him my food when my mother wasn't looking.

I longed for her love and affection. When continuously making the honor roll didn't get her attention, I got involved in other extracurricular activities. She once told me she had played softball. So I began playing basketball, volleyball, and running track. And I was good at all of them. But she never saw her baby girl play in even one game. I finished fourth overall in my middle school, but I couldn't tell if she was proud or not. The beatings started again. There were times I didn't want to dress out in physical education because of the bruises left behind by the belt or extension cord.

By the time I started high school, my attitude was: *If my mother doesn't care about me, why should I care about myself?* During my freshman year I got into multiple fights and failed algebra and Spanish. I was fourteen the last time my mother beat me. I stood there and took every hit from the extension cord, each cutting the skin on my arms, on my legs. I thought: *Really? A beating?* I would not give her the satisfaction of seeing me cry. Lord knows it was painful. I had goosebumps, and my breathing was hurried. I just stared her in the face and took every hit. I had my fists balled up by my side, wanting to hit her. When it was over, I left home and went to live with a relative who was like a mother to me.

During that time I made all of my own decisions, good or bad. I was angry all the time. I got suspended for fighting and skipped school to be with my boyfriend since eighth grade. My aunt would sign me back into school because my mother stopped talking to me after I had moved out.

By my sophomore year, I came to the realization that self-afflicted pain and self-destruction was not the solution to my problems. My grandmother had always told us that in order to succeed in life, we needed an education. I enrolled in business classes and had plans of becoming a certified public accountant. I excelled in my accounting classes, receiving all As. I was amazed at how compiling receipts and other documents and making sense out of them reminded me of how I grew up: taking adversity and making sense out of it.

But then during my senior year I became pregnant by my boyfriend. I was seventeen and still angry much of the time. I almost had a fight when I was pregnant! But I thought about my unborn child and walked away. My dreams of playing on the varsity basketball team and receiving an advanced honors diploma with a concentration in business were replaced with going to night school, graduating a semester early with a general diploma and getting a job when my son was only a month old. I was determined not to end up like my mother and go on welfare.

The following September my grandmother died unexpectedly from a heart attack. Without my biggest fan, I didn't know where to turn. I tried to keep working and started dating someone new. When we broke up, I stopped working and found myself following the same path as my mother; I ended up on welfare and living back in the Butler Housing Projects. Some would say I was living a generational curse: living day-to-day without a plan.

I tried going to junior college but couldn't focus. My grandmother would have turned over in her grave if she knew I was living like a projects chick. Even though I was raised in the projects, my grandmother didn't raise us with a projects mentality.

She would say, "It's not where you live; it's how you live."

She raised us to be independent and make a way out of no way, not to depend on a check from the government.

After being shot at by a jealous baby momma, and almost shooting her with a 12 gauge shotgun, I decided I didn't want to die in the streets or let someone else dictate my behavior. I remembered how my grandmother advised my eldest cousin to join the military. Grateful that she had planted that seed, I took my grandmother's advice and joined the military to make a better life for me and my son. I did have a few fights in basic training. But receiving a dishonorable discharge was not an option, so I learned how to control my anger. I focused on being a better person and, most importantly, being a better role model for my son.

While in the military I got married to give my son the childhood I never had; a mother and a father. At first I was very protective of my son because of all that I had seen as a child. It's hard to erase our past, but I knew I had to at least move past it and accept it as a part of my journey.

I had reservations when my husband wanted to discipline him or told me how to discipline him. I never wanted my son to talk to me through a door. I didn't make the same mistake in choosing a partner that my mother had. Not only did my husband show my son how a father should treat a son, he also showed me how a man should treat a woman with a child. I needed that.

I worked full-time as a soldier, mother, and wife. I earned my associate degree and started on my bachelor's. Shortly after receiving an honorable discharge from the Army, I became a law enforcement officer, which is my greatest accomplishment.

As a law enforcement officer, I work directly with the community I serve. I'm not just an enforcer of the law; I am a mentor and a role model to the youth in my community. Having a similar background to the youth I come in contact with, I can relate to their generational scars and provide guidance and assistance to steer them away from the criminal justice system.

I consider myself an example of how to not be a product of your environment. As an officer assigned to public housing, I tell them what my grandmother told me: *It's not where you live; it's how you live.*

As a school resource officer, I stress the importance of getting an education and getting along with your peers. As a basketball coach for our Police Athletic League, I work with the forgotten youth in our community who are at-risk from lack of parenting and other socioeconomic factors.

I know my passion and love for education helped me build character, so seeing the youth I work with graduate from high school and turn their lives around makes me proud. Even angry parents of juveniles I have arrested, thank me for caring enough to follow up with their child when I see them in the community.

Having a job that I love and being appreciated is my greatest accomplishment. Despite working ten-to twelve-hour days, I still find time to volunteer with the PTA and as a youth advisor at church. My life experiences have without a doubt molded me into a compassionate person willing to advocate for others. I have made an impact in my community as an intelligent, capable, dedicate, personable professional. As the executive director of the Police Athletic League, I learned a lot about running a nonprofit. I used this knowledge and skill to start my own business, Jada's Prints, a custom apparel business. My long-term goal is to partner with a school or technical center and teach youth how to make an honest living decorating apparel, instilling the same work ethic and character I have acquired while preparing them for the workplace or to become entrepreneurs themselves.

More than anything, I want to be a living example that troubled beginnings don't always lead to tragedy; life is about choices and self-accountability. Abuse can become achievements. Poverty can become power. It's time to change!

About the Author

Sherrie L Johnson is a dedicated mother of three biological children—Nickolaus, Kori, and Layla-Simone—and a mother figure to several others. As a member of Third Baptist Church, she has served on the Youth Ministry and the Women's Ministry. Sherrie is a US Army veteran and a seventeen-year law enforcement officer with the local police department where she was recently promoted to a Patrol Sergeant in the Uniform Field Operations Division becoming the first black female to attain this position. She earned an associatedegree from Saint Leo University, a bachelor's degree from Virginia State University, and has completed her firstyear at Concord Law School.

She was voted class president of the Fifty-Seventh Basic Police Academy, executive director of the Petersburg Police Athletic League, president of the Fraternal Order of Police, Lodge No. 16, and served on the Virginia PTA board of managers as the James River District Director.

Please visit bit.ly/nmc2freebie to receive your 11 Ways Youth Can Become Agents of Change guide

Conclusion

No matter how your life has unfolded so far, every single thing you have experienced has been valuable and necessary for shaping you into the person you are destined to become.

No matter how challenging. How hard. How tough. Life wants to you expand. And sometimes that expansion comes through challenge, or heartache, or loss, or struggle.

Know that it all has been divinely orchestrated because life loves you. So take a moment to give thanks and appreciation for everything your pain has brought you so far, no matter how tough.

Acknowledge all the beautiful inner growth and transformation you have experienced and remember that is way more important than what it looks like from the outside. And then take a deep breath and release whatever you no longer want to carry so you can get ready to enjoy what the rest of your life has to offer.

The thing about change is that in order for things around you to change, you have to change.

Action Step #1: Recognize That the Problem Is Not Outside of You; It's Inside of You.

Perception is projection. We don't see things as they are; we see them as *we* are.

The way we perceive the world determines the world we project around us. This means we have the ability to change the reality we are projecting simply by changing how we see it.

Every thing, event, and person is neutral. It just is. And then we come along and place a label on it—good or bad, right or wrong, positive or negative. We also make it mean something.

Your true power lies in not necessarily changing your reality but in changing the way you are experiencing your reality. Change the way you are labeling the events, people, or circumstances in your life. And most importantly, changing what you are making these events mean about *you*.

The way we perceive the world is based on how our beliefs, our memories, our thoughts, and our emotions combine together to create our stories, the chain of thoughts that typically play through our minds about the different areas of our lives.

The problem is that many of us have come to believe that our stories are true. We have spent our entire life accruing evidence from our world to support them. Because we have perceived the world through our stories, we have in turn created a world that reflects our stories.

Once you realize that everything you're telling yourself is just a story, you now have a choice.

You can choose how you perceive your world. You can choose to perceive your world in a way that supports and empowers you rather than in a way that limits and disempowers you.

Action Step #2: Heal Your Relationship with Yourself; Heal Your Relationship with Others.

It's time to take a deep look inwards.

We all have a nasty inner critic who not only attacks us but also attacks others. I encourage you to change your relationship with your inner critic and start transforming it into your inner cheerleader.

The inner critic judges, blames, compares, shames, and criticizes. Whereas the inner cheerleader just loves unconditionally and freely, and this type of love does not need to be earned.

Our inner critic is driven by fear, while our inner cheerleader is the voice of love. Fear cannot dim the light of love, yet the light of love will completely outshine the darkness of fear.

We heal all fears and shame through love, embracing them and opening up to them. Every time we push against our fear-driven inner critic, we actually strengthen that voice within us.

This step is about beginning to see your inner critic not as your enemy but rather as a part of you crying for love. The fear voice is simply a light that shows you an area of yourself not being loved.

The areas of yourself and your life that the inner critic attacks the most are the areas that require the most love from you.

This is not about eliminating your inner critic but rather changing your relationship with it. You have the ability to change how you respond to it.

Action Step #3: Master the Art of Manifestation.

The key to mastering manifestation is to understand that everything is energy.

Everything that you see in your world—whether it is a piece of furniture, money, or your body—is simply a mass of vibrating energy that has come together to form matter. If you put any of these things under a very strong microscope, all you will see is a mass of atoms and molecules buzzing together.

Yes, this concept can mess with your head a little initially; however, once grasped it will support you in the process of manifesting what you desire.

The next thing for you to understand is that energy can vibrate at different rates: a high/fast vibration or a low/slow vibration.

To explain this let's use water as an example. When you heat water, you cause the atoms that comprise water to vibrate at a faster rate. This changes the form of the water, and it turns to steam.

But when you freeze water, you slow down the vibration of the atom's energy within the water, which makes it denser and creates ice.

The most powerful way to apply this principle is understanding that you can hold your body in a high and light vibration or in a low and slow vibration.

Thinking positive, happy thoughts raises your vibration and makes the energy in your body vibrate at a higher rate that creates more positive emotions. This in turn attracts more positive and good things to you.

Thinking negative, sad thoughts makes the energy in your body vibrate at a lower rate, creating more negative emotion. This in turn attracts more negative things to you.

Action Step #4: Script a New Story for Your Life.

Mindset is everything. It's easy to say change your mindset, but how do we do that? Do we snap our fingers then *boom*, our mindset is instantly changed? Not really. You have to constantly focus on keeping yourself in a positive, receptive energy to allow what you want to come to you. You also have to focus on how you want things to be instead of how they are now.

Get two pieces of lined paper to write about what you desire for your life. Write this in the present tense as if it's true. Describe each area of your life as you want it to be. Describe how you will feel when you are living this.

This is your new story. This is the story you are going to begin to tell yourself about your life. Next, try this exercise that I have recently incorporated into my own life, and I love it. I highly recommend you try it and commit to it.

Desire Creation Audio Track

Record an audio track describing your dream life and telling yourself that you can have it. This will be something that you can listen to everyday.

1) Choose a method to record your audio. Options include:
    Garage Band software (on a mac)
    Download Audacity http://audacity.sourceforge.net/
    Voice memo app on your iPhone.

2) Take your desire script from worksheet 1 and read it out loud. You can either read it like: *I am living my dream life. Every day I wake up and… etc.* Or you can read it as though you are talking to yourself: *Self, you are living your dream life. Every day you wake up and … etc.* It's up to you.

3) Personalize this audio. You can say positive and empowering affirmations to yourself. You can paint a picture of how it will feel when you have these desires. You can even tell yourself all of the reasons why this is possible. Include whatever you like!

4) This is about you creating something where every day you can hear your own voice affirming that everything you desire is coming to you. You will hear your own voice telling you what it's like to live your dream life.

5) Once you have recorded the audio, put it on your iPod and set aside time each day to listen to it. If you cannot set aside dedicated, listen to it on your way to work or while making dinner.

6) Update your track as often as you want to. Add in more details or as your desires manifest you may want to record new ones to reflect the new dreams you are dreaming.

Action Step #5: Heal with Love

Tune into your heart and ask yourself: *What would it look like if I loved and accepted myself just as I am? What would be different? What actions would I be taking?*

Describe it and journal it.

This is a really powerful practice to turn down the voice of your inner critic and help you start redeveloping a loving and beautiful relationship with yourself.

I want you to imagine what you looked like as a little four-year-old. If you cannot remember, find an old photograph.

1. Close your eyes. Create a clear picture on the screen of your mind of what you looked like. What was your hair like? Your skin? Your eyes? What are you wearing?

2. Imagine yourself at the age you are now. You can see the little four-year-old. What is she doing? Where is she? Is she at school or at home? How is she feeling?

3. Approach her. As you move closer to her, notice her reaction. Does she want to come and talk to you or play with you? Or does she run away? Whatever she wants to do, just allow her to do it.

4. When she is ready, ask her to come and sit on your lap so that you can talk to her. Take some time to see how she is. Ask her questions to find out how she is feeling, or if there is anything she needs. If she is not happy, ask her what she needs from you in order to feel happy.

5. Now give her love. Show her love in whatever way you want whether it is by cuddling her, kissing her, singing to her, or playing with her. Notice the feeling that comes up in you as you give her love.

6. Stay with this. Keep giving her love. Feel the feeling of love inside you.

7. Now allow her to guide you through the rest of the exercise. She may

want you to stay with her and play. She may want to say goodbye, so she can do her own thing. Or she may want to stay cuddling you. Allow her to show you what she wants and needs.

8. When you're finished stay sitting with your eyes closed and notice the emotions that are inside of you. Notice the feeling of love inside of you. This is what it feels like to love yourself. You do not need to do anything or be anything. You are already deserving of love just as you are.

Anytime you want to reconnect with love for yourself, imagine you are with your child self. Send her love. Send yourself love.

It's Time for Change

There are no limits to what you can create and experience in this lifetime. When you tap into your true power and release all of the limiting beliefs holding you back, you will be invincible.

Now it is time to live big. It is time to live your dreams. Use the space below to write down everything you can do to transform that dream into a reality. Write down everything you can think of.

If you had unlimited confidence, unlimited self-love, and believed in yourself 100 percent, what steps would you be taking? What brave, bold action steps could you follow through on that would lead you to your grand five-year vision? Declare them on paper.

Where to from here?

It's time to shine your light and show the world who you are. Take on board everything you have learned or discovered and step forward into the world with a brave heart and bold ambitions.

Revisit these worksheets, action steps, and stories whenever you need support. Use the exercises and practices you have learned whenever you need a boost.

Stay connected with our tribe through the My Story Has Purpose Facebook community and keep sharing yourself with the people who are here to support you.

If you have some feedback on your experiences, or if you would like to share with me what you achieved, I would love to hear from you. Please email me at info@arisquires.com.

You Are Amazing!

www.ingramcontent.com/pod-product-compliance
Lightning Source LLC
Chambersburg PA
CBHW052053070526
44584CB00017B/2158